# Founding
— to —
Finishing

# Founding
— to —
# Finishing

A 40-YEAR JOURNEY
*of* STARTING AND LEADING
A NONPROFIT

Edwin J. Staub

Copyright © 2024 by Edwin J. Staub

All rights reserved. No part of this book may be reproduced or used in any manner without written permission of the copyright owner except for the use of quotations in a book review.

Scripture quotations taken from the following Bible translations:

Holy Bible, New International Version, NIV. Copyright © 1973, 1978, 1984, 2011 by Biblica, Inc. All rights reserved.

Holy Bible, New Living Translation, copyright © 1996, 2005, 2015 by Tyndall House Foundation. Used by permission of Tyndale House Publishers. All rights reserved.

Holy Bible, Common English Version, Copyright © 2019 Common English Bible Committee. All rights reserved.

First printing 2024

Book and cover designed by Burtch Hunter

Printed in Canada

ISBN 979-8-218-50861-6

*In memory of Jean Parks,
my long-time executive assistant,
who set the standard for excellence,
professionalism, and kindness.*

# CONTENTS

ACKNOWLEDGMENTS ................................................. ix
INTRODUCTION ...................................................... 1
TIMELINE ............................................................ 5

## SEASON ONE: FOUNDING

*Founding Thoughts* ................................................ 11
Setting the Cornerstone .......................................... 13
Defining Your Mission ............................................ 37

## SEASON TWO: LEADING

*Leading Thoughts* ................................................ 69
Launching Your Mission ........................................... 73
Living a Mission-Led Culture ..................................... 93
Maintaining and Growing Your Mission ............................ 103

## SEASON THREE: FINISHING

*Finishing Thoughts* ............................................. 117
Planning for Succession ......................................... 119
The Search ...................................................... 133
Making a Successful Transition .................................. 147
Closing Perspectives ............................................ 165

EPILOGUE ......................................................... 177

# ACKNOWLEDGMENTS

AS my leadership transition neared, I was often asked what my next "season" would look like. I can still remember sharing with several people that it would not entail writing another book! I have since been reminded of that comment as we have invested countless hours in *Founding to Finishing*. It has become a God-inspired project.

First, I want to thank my wife, Kayanne. She has been an incredible inspiration and confidant throughout my Eagle Ranch journey.

Secondly, I am grateful to the Ranch's Director of Communications, Stefanie Long, and board member Mart Martin who encouraged me to write this book, believing there were some valuable insights that could benefit others. Stefanie spent many hours organizing my thoughts and research into a coherent flow.

Thanks as well to Kris Peters, my former executive assistant, who typed many early drafts that were illegible both to her and to me, and Jessica Sweeney, who reorganized and edited many renditions. Her tenacity and professionalism kept this project moving forward.

A special thanks to John Vardeman, the author of our first book, *On Eagle's Wings,* for his invaluable editing of this book to ensure it preserved "my voice." He is one of the most gifted writers I know.

Thanks to Tim Irwin, who was instrumental in Eagle Ranch's search for my successor and whose insights in the transition process were pivotal.

And to Pat MacMillan, a mentor of 30 years, whose wisdom and investment in me and so many others will impact generations.

To my dear friend Jim Webb, who passed away in 2019 and was a guiding light for me from the earliest days of Eagle Ranch. His thoughtful candor kept me in the guardrails as a young founder.

To my successor, John Shackelford, a gracious servant leader and God's man for such a time as this.

To my former and current board of directors and advisors, who have not only become friends but whose ownership of the Ranch mission has been inspirational. Their wisdom is represented throughout this book.

To Eagle Ranch staff, past and present, for your willingness to take a road less traveled to serve the children and mission of Eagle Ranch. Future staff will stand on your shoulders.

To my wonderful family. Eagle Ranch would be much less than it is today without their encouragement in ways they will never know. Thank you for being a place of joy and rest for me during my 40-year journey.

And finally, to Jesus, who gives life meaning and purpose. Eagle Ranch exists for His glory.

# INTRODUCTION

## Why This Book?

PROVERBS 15:22 says, "*Plans fail for lack of counsel, but with many advisors they succeed.*" When I am asked about the success of Eagle Ranch over the years, I cite that verse as one of the pivotal reasons.

We are all myopic to some extent, and our outlook regarding vision, systems, and processes is limited. So many times, Eagle Ranch staff, our board of directors and advisors, and other trusted confidants have been instrumental in keeping our mission within the guardrails and moving forward. My hope is that this book will, in some ways, be a trusted advisor as your missional calling unfolds.

I wrote this book to capture in themes and concepts what I've learned over our history that might be helpful to others on their journey in the nonprofit sector and perhaps in the for-profit arena as well.

This is not an exhaustive narrative on best practice but one containing what I would consider "barge turners," seemingly small ideas that can move the rudder in such a way to significantly impact and, in some cases, redirect a mission.

I have completed my season with Eagle Ranch—from founding the Ranch in the early 1980s to passing the baton to the next generation of leadership in 2021.

Certain milestones in founding a nonprofit organization to finishing well are unique but, in many ways, still consistent in the lifespan of any organization. If even a few of these areas resonate with you and become barge turners for your organization, the investment in writing this book will have been worthwhile.

## A Road Less Traveled

On February 5, 2021, I sat across the table at a local restaurant from a young man who sensed a calling in his life to leave behind a comfortable, promising career and follow God's path for him and his family.

I felt in many ways that I was looking in a mirror. Forty years earlier, I had made a similar decision. We both came from stable families and privileged backgrounds, played college athletics, and, as youths, were "old souls" who appreciated traditional values. Most significantly, we had a heart for those who struggled in life.

What began as a one-hour lunch grew much longer. I felt that I was speaking with a kindred spirit in a God-

## INTRODUCTION

appointed space and time. Six months later, this young man, John Shackelford, would start his own journey as the new leader of Eagle Ranch.

*Founding to Finishing* chronicles my calling, alongside a committed board and staff, in starting a nonprofit from scratch, leading it through four decades, and, by God's grace, finishing well.

I hope the honesty and transparency in the following pages will encourage and challenge you on your own unique journey.

Abandonment to a cause greater than ourselves is where we begin. This is our story.

## To Look Forward, We Must First Look Backward

When I first arrived in Georgia in 1982, with almost no resources, I wrote down this quote on a napkin: *"Attempt something so great for God that it is doomed to failure unless God be in it."* (John Haggai). That napkin is now framed and displayed as a constant reminder of the "why," or purpose, behind Eagle Ranch.

First, that Eagle Ranch would be a tangible expression of God's goodness and power in this world. I have been so encouraged that when people look at Eagle Ranch, they don't see me or a group of individuals but they see a God who does great things in this world. The

God of Abraham, Isaac, and Jacob is still alive and moving His Kingdom forward.

The second aspect of our why is to embody Jesus to children who have lost their way and communicate the ancient and timeless verse, Jeremiah 29:11. *"For I know the plans I have for you, declares the Lord, plans to prosper you and not to harm you, plans to give you hope and a future."* What a great privilege to intersect another person's story and communicate that truth.

Eagle Ranch started as a humble dream in 1985 as a home for boys who were hurting and had lost hope for their futures. Today, the Ranch has grown well past that initial home for eight boys and even beyond being just a residential program. It has become a robust Christ-centered organization committed to helping restore and renew children and families in a myriad of ways.

As we have innovated and grown, we have always looked back to our why to make sure this innovation is consistent with who we've said we are from the earliest days of Eagle Ranch. Our greatest passion is to communicate God's love in our community and beyond.

LEARN MORE ABOUT EAGLE RANCH AND ITS MISSION OF WHOLE FAMILY HEALING.

# TIMELINE

THIS timeline outlines key historical dates in the growth and development of Eagle Ranch. It demonstrates that an organization positioned to stand the test of time never opens its doors fully developed. Growth comes with wise counsel, experience, and the establishment of a trustworthy reputation. "Need drives vision" has been a historical mantra for us—our dream expands as synergistic needs in our community emerge.

It is important to note that Eagle Ranch has been a debt-free organization since its inception. Facilities and programs added throughout our history were funded beforehand. Trusting that God will provide for our needs has proven true time and again and is a tangible expression of our reliance on Him to set the pace of our growth.

1982 — Eddie Staub arrives in Georgia

1983 — Contract signed on Eagle Ranch land

1984 — John W. Jacobs Administration Building

1985 — First boy arrives (April 13th); Faith Home

1986 — Hope Home (2nd boys' home)

## Founding to Finishing

1987 — Love Home (3rd boys' home)

1988 — Peace Home (4th boys' home)

1993 — Chapel in the Woods

1995 — W. E. Reeve and T. L. Foley Athletic Center

1996 — Wilheit Administration and Counseling Center

1997 — Wings Consulting program initiated; Grace Home and Joy Home (5th & 6th boys' homes)

2001 — First girl arrives at Eagle Ranch; Glory Home and Praise Home (1st & 2nd girls' homes); Launch of Eagle Ranch School (modular units)

2006 — Completion of permanent Eagle Ranch School facility

2009 — Wink Wynne Lodge, a gathering place for our Ranch family and special events; Blessing Home and Mercy Home (3rd & 4th girls' homes)

2014 — Whitcomb Family Equine Program launched

2019 — Joan Whitcomb Girls' Wellness and Activity Center

2021 — John Shackelford appointed to succeed Founder Eddie Staub as Executive Director

2022 — Eddie Staub develops and leads The James W. Webb Wings Center, an outpatient counseling and retreat center, and the new home to Wings Consulting, a nonprofit mentoring initiative.

# Founding
— to —
Finishing

SEASON ONE

# Founding

Eddie Staub and his dog, Connor. 1984

## *Founding Thoughts*

WHEN I first arrived in Georgia in the early 1980s, I had a credibility challenge to say the least. I was from another state, knew no one in Georgia, and was communicating with anyone who would listen about my God-inspired mission to start Eagle Ranch. (I learned later that someone had even called Auburn University and spoken to the Dean of Students to confirm that I actually attended and played baseball there.)

After being in Georgia about six months, one of our earliest supporters, Loyd Strickland, arranged a meeting for me with his good friend Sonny Ellis, who was retiring as CFO of Genuine Parts. The purpose of this meeting was for me to share my ambitious plans with Mr. Ellis, a highly respected businessman in the Atlanta corporate and foundation communities.

In advance of our meeting, Mr. Ellis asked me to bring my business plan for Eagle Ranch. Although I didn't articulate it at the time, I wondered, "What is a business plan?" My first thought was that it probably had to do with how much it was going to take to operate and develop the Ranch.

My meeting with Mr. Ellis was on May 9, 1983, at 4:30 p.m. After some initial conversation, he asked if he could see my business plan. I took my one page "plan" out of my briefcase and passed it across the desk. In retrospect, I can almost see, even today, this Southern gentleman trying to hide his shock and surprise. After what seemed like an eternity, he passed the sheet back across the desk and said the most encouraging words that have ever been spoken to me in all my years at Eagle Ranch.

"Eddie, what you want to do is impossible, but I'm not taking into account what God can do through you and others."

Those simple words echoed my deepest heart's resolve in starting Eagle Ranch: When the Ranch became a reality, it wouldn't be about me or anyone else, but it would be about God and His glory.

# Setting the Cornerstone

## Foundational Reflections

My founding dream started as a young boy. I had several experiences throughout my youth into early adulthood where I witnessed young people who faced struggles. It always stirred a question deep within: "Why them and not me?"

As long as I can remember, I was always struck by the reality that the grace of God was the only reason that I had what I had growing up. And it was out of gratitude for God's goodness to me that I wanted to help others less fortunate.

Nearly 40 years after starting Eagle Ranch, I'm still grateful. I'm also a lot wiser.

Founding a nonprofit organization is not for the faint of heart. Equally daunting is handing the reins over to someone else after pouring so much of your heart and soul into an endeavor.

As I look back on my journey, there were many milestones, warning signals, redirections and steps of faith along the way.

When I was about to leave Alabama to start Eagle Ranch at the age of 27, I thought that this undertaking would have a high probability of failure. Then, I began to think that if I were at the end of my life and had never tried, would I regret it? The answer was a resounding "yes."

On a more humorous note, a Franciscan nun in Alabama named Mother Angelica had started a Catholic network after leaving her comfortable life in Chicago. She was quite a rebel and had heard about my desire to start Eagle Ranch. I'll never forget meeting with Mother Angelica. She looked at me and said, "Eddie Staub, do you know what faith is?" I thought she was about to quote some well-known scriptures on faith. Instead, she said, "Faith is having one foot on the ground, one foot in the air, and a sick feeling in your stomach." How true that statement was!

SEASON ONE: FOUNDING

> *If I were at the end of my life and had never tried, would I regret it?*

## Founding Considerations

The thoughts shared in the following section are lessons I experienced firsthand, some of which I think I have done well while others I wish I could redo. These are not exhaustive lessons, but ones I believe were pivotal in my journey to start Eagle Ranch.

*Founding* is a loaded word. Laying a foundation is just one part of the process, yet arguably the most important. When I look back to the key influences and experiences that shepherded my journey, there are principles on founding that are important to share.

These founding thoughts speak to the heart of a leader responsible for the crucial work of bringing vision to life. Consider this a primer to help you ask deeper questions and identify the lessons that will emerge as you begin, or continue, your own journey.

The following pages explore areas I believe are fundamental to every founder's ability to succeed:

- Preparation
- Stepping Out
- Motives
- Passion
- Remembrance
- Principles
- Persistence

SEASON ONE: FOUNDING

# Preparation

I believe God's revelation to us is progressive. There are those Pauline "Damascus Road" experiences—when God's purpose is immediate and unmistakable—but I believe those to be more the exception than the rule. As I look back over my life's story, I can see numerous instances that prepared me as a founder of a children's program.

As early as eight years old, I felt a God-given burden to help hurting people. I was raised in a home of simplicity, a strong work ethic, discipline and, most of all, a reverence for the transcendence and sovereignty of God.

Through my college baseball career and vigorous graduate studies, I developed perseverance. I gained hands-on experience working at another children's home doing every job imaginable from physical plant to caring for children to overseeing staff. Later, I was drawn into solitude and loneliness with the Lord as this vision of Eagle Ranch began to take shape.

Forty years later, it all makes sense.

Looking back, I can now connect the dots. Throughout my life, I had interests and experiences that would lead me to the *dreaming* and then the *doing* required to bring Eagle Ranch to life. God cleared a path, but I only saw the "next step" along the way.

A lot of preparation for your life's calling ends up being based on things you didn't plan or control—they just happened. But if you take the time to reflect on key moments in your life, you might just see beyond those one-by-one steps that led you to where you are today.

> ### KEY LESSON
>
> God doesn't waste our experiences even if we feel at the time they are not related with anything that we want to do. It may seem like just a smorgasbord of experiences that don't add up. But many times in our lives, to look forward we must first look backward.
>
> *How has God prepared you through your life experiences for this calling?*

## Stepping Out

I believe when you surrender your life to God, He takes you up on it. I started my career in childcare at Big Oak Ranch in Gadsden, Alabama. John Croyle, the founder, played football for Bear Bryant at the University of Alabama. A charismatic and gifted speaker, he is four years older than me, and during my college days at Auburn University, I was drawn to him as a mentor. My whole intent

SEASON ONE: FOUNDING

was to be John's assistant as his Big Oak dream unfolded.

However, after almost a year, I was beginning to feel pulled to leave Big Oak. I didn't want to go, and I certainly felt inadequate to accomplish anything close to what John had done in Gadsden. I had had very few accolades on the athletic field as a former Auburn baseball player and no connections outside of Birmingham. But God had other plans, and His Spirit was making me more and more uncomfortable staying at Big Oak Ranch. I almost felt compelled to leave.

I remember saying to God, "You have the wrong person." I didn't feel I had the giftedness or even the faith to leave. As I felt more called to start my own children's program, I did what many people do when God leads them outside their comfort zone: bargain. My fallback plea was, "Okay, I'll do this, but I'm not leaving my home state."

So, my first step into this calling was to research the need for a children's home in Alabama. I scoured the whole state, from as far north as Huntsville to Mobile in the south. In the midst of seeking, I learned that although there wasn't a need in Alabama, there was a need in Northeast Georgia. The problem was I had no money, land, or direct contacts in Georgia.

While this discovery was discouraging and made me question my calling, I realize now it was a test of my conviction. It gave me an opportunity to discern if I was willing to step out in faith.

> ### KEY LESSON
>
> Isaiah 55:8 states, *"'My plans are not your plans, nor are your ways my ways,' says the Lord."* Feeling drawn to a cause or a mission doesn't always mean your plans will come together neatly or conveniently. You may be led into an area of need where you have no connections or resources.
>
> *Your calling may lead you to unexpected, uncomfortable, and unprepared places. Are you willing to step out in faith?*

## Motives

A question I'm most often asked is, "What was the hardest thing about founding Eagle Ranch?" The answer most people expect is usually one of the following: financial challenges, building credibility, locating property, or enlisting others in my vision.

But without a doubt, my biggest struggle was determining my motives for wanting to engage in this undertaking. Unfortunately, that soul searching did not begin until after I had already arrived in Georgia to start Eagle Ranch. I can't remember why I felt this was so important

SEASON ONE: FOUNDING

at that particular time, but I was really convicted in my spirit about looking inward.

At the time, I was living at Ignatius House, a spiritual retreat center in north Atlanta. For two days, I went down to their little chapel and wrestled with God about why I wanted to start Eagle Ranch. I went into this process not knowing what the end result would be, but it was a necessary exercise of humility and openness to God's plan.

As you can imagine, I had all kinds of conflicting thoughts in examining my motives. I had already told people in Alabama and Georgia what I was doing. To exit this journey because my motives were ego-driven or self-serving would be humiliating, but it was a process I was convinced needed to be pursued.

I came out of those days with a bit of an epiphany. First, my motives were not 100 percent pure in starting Eagle Ranch, and they never would be. Ego, pride, and wanting to prove myself were mixed in with my core desire, which was to glorify God and be the hands and feet of Jesus to children who didn't have the opportunities I did.

I was quite befuddled by this outcome and called a good friend of mine, Randy Pope, who started Perimeter Church in Atlanta. I shared with him my anguish in not having pure motives, to which he simply replied, "Eddie, join the human race." What an incredible relief that was to me, and the journey for Eagle Ranch really began at that point.

*Without a doubt, my biggest struggle was determining my motives.*

SEASON ONE: FOUNDING

> ### KEY LESSON
>
> It is worth the intense introspection to determine if your calling to a mission is truly God-inspired. If your list of motives doesn't include some selfish aspects, it's probably not an honest assessment. It would be difficult to be passionate about a mission that didn't fulfill some personal desire. But your core, anchoring motive should be something that addresses a need beyond your own.
>
> *What are some of the motives driving*
> *your actions and pursuits?*
> *Does your core motive serve a purpose*
> *outside of yourself?*

## Passion

Dealing with people's skepticism about my starting Eagle Ranch was a challenge. But it was never disheartening, which is a bit odd given the insensitivity and veracity of many comments I received day in and day out. I was emboldened by the knowledge that God was with me and that He was confirming my calling in His own time and own way.

On August 30, 1982, at 10:30 a.m., I met with Victor Gregory, Vice President of External Affairs for Trust Company, an iconic financial institution in Atlanta. Vic had seen it all. People who were very effective as nonprofit leaders, those who weren't, and those who were dreamers. I am afraid I landed in that latter category.

Victor was very kind to me during our half-hour meeting but had conveniently "scheduled" a lunch, so our time was quickly coming to an end. Victor, the quintessential Southern gentleman, was very cordial. However, I felt he was struggling to believe Eagle Ranch would ever become a reality.

As our meeting was wrapping up, I turned to him and said something like, "I am going to start Eagle Ranch and when it happens, it won't be because of me, but because God wants this to be built in Georgia. I will do this with or without you." I think I even shocked myself, and I could tell Victor paused. He looked at me and said, "Sit back down and let's talk some more."

Victor became one of our greatest advocates in the Atlanta business community in those crucial early days. He believed in my passion to undertake what many felt was an impossible task.

I had a similar visit with University of Georgia Head Football Coach Vince Dooley when I first arrived in Georgia. My message to Vince was, "Coach, I'm 27 years old,

SEASON ONE: FOUNDING

> *I was emboldened by the knowledge that God was with me.*

and all I have is a dream to give struggling boys a home. I don't have any money, I don't have any land, and I don't know anyone in Georgia. I am asking you to stick your neck out for me."

Vince, like Victor, paused for an uncomfortable length of time. He finally looked at me and said, "Eddie, anything you need, you let me know."

### KEY LESSON

My early meetings and interactions with others taught me that if you don't believe in yourself and your dream, how can you expect others to? People respond to mission but even more so to passion.

*Why do you have a passion for your particular undertaking?*
*How can you clearly and concisely articulate that passion so others can understand it?*

## Remembrance

Throughout my journey in starting Eagle Ranch, I felt very much like a pilgrim. There was a real sense that it was just God and me. As I was about to leave Alabama for Georgia, I didn't know where I was going to stay. With limited funds, lodging was a very important concern.

My mother suggested calling Father John Schroeder who started Ignatius House. She mentioned that Father Schroeder had studied with my father in the Jesuit track in the early 1950s. Fortunately, Father Schroeder was very open to taking in "Brother's" son for two months. I had a free place to stay!

With only one week left in my allotted time at Ignatius House, I had nowhere to go. Then I ran into the only person I knew in Atlanta, David Salyers, who worked for Chick-fil-A. David asked me what I was doing in Atlanta, and I told him what I wanted to do. He then asked me where I was staying, and I said, "Well I know where I am staying for another week, and then I don't know." David's face lit up and he said, "Eddie, there's a friend of mine at Chick-fil-A who is moving to North Carolina and needs someone to house-sit in Powder Springs for six months." I had my second place to stay!

This pattern occurred four more times. Often, I didn't know where I would stay the following night. The importance of this, even today, is that it serves as a reminder of God's provision in the midst of difficult or impossible circumstances.

> **KEY LESSON**
>
> I have always believed that remembrance is the key to faith, and those early days will give you a strong foundation of remembrance. God doesn't change, and the God who was with me in the early 1980s continues to provide today.
>
> *When and where have you experienced God's provision in a miraculous way?*

## Principles

Staying dependent on God's path for you can be especially difficult when you have so many opportunities to "relieve the pain" of the challenges confronting you at every turn.

In our early days, a foundation from out of state was in the process of awarding a significant grant to Eagle Ranch that would have been a tremendous boost for us. In the final weeks before the grant was to be made, the executive director called and said that the foundation didn't give to religious organizations. He went on to say that if we could rewrite our proposal stating that our Christian faith was not our primary focus, then this generous grant would be ours. I shared with him that Christ was central to everything we did and understood that stance would eliminate us from consideration. The end of the conversation was very cordial, but in my mind, it was the end of that opportunity.

I know the world is becoming increasingly hostile to things that are Christian, but if I claim the name of Christ, I need to be able to stand up to that criticism and accept the consequences that go along with my profession of faith.

Interestingly, I received a call a week later from that executive director, who said his trustees were so impressed that we stood up for our beliefs—even at a great cost—that they wanted to make the grant anyway.

Another challenging decision was when two separate groups wanted to *give* us land, but these two land parcels were not in an area of the greatest need. One group went so far as to say that if we took the land they offered, all our operational expenses and needs would be underwritten in perpetuity. Both opportunities looked on the surface like the very provision I had prayed for, but I knew in my heart that this was not what God wanted for Eagle Ranch.

I distinctly remember calling each group, expressing gratitude for their thoughtfulness but letting them know we would not be able to proceed with their kind offers. After those phone calls, I almost physically felt my dependence, which had subtly become aligned with those two groups, shift back to God. Shortly thereafter, we located the land on which Eagle Ranch is now situated.

A *Harvard Business Review* article by Clayton Christensen shared this about living a principle-based life:

*In theory, surely I could have crossed over the line just that one time and then not done it again. But looking back on it, resisting the temptation whose logic was, 'In this extenuating circumstance, just this once, it's OK' has proven to be one of the most important decisions of my life. Why? My life has been one unending stream of extenuating circumstances. Had I crossed that line that one time, I would have done it over and over in the years that followed.*

*The lesson I learned from this is that it's easier to hold on to your principles 100 percent of the time than it is to hold on to them 98 percent of the time. If you give in to 'just this once,' based on marginal cost analysis, as some of my former classmates have done, you'll regret where you end up. You've got to define for yourself what you stand for and draw the line in a safe place.*

I have consistently seen that compromising is a slippery slope. There will always be a "just this once," and then it becomes an ongoing battle to keep the original line you drew for yourself from eroding.

SEASON ONE: FOUNDING

### KEY LESSON

Don't compromise your principles on even the smallest detail. Stay true to who you are and to God's way in all things. You may have to say "no" to great opportunities, even those that seem divinely provided. It will pay dividends not just in the present but in the future too.

*Have you shifted any of your plans
because of outside influences?
What are the areas of "no compromise" for you?*

## Persistence

We face all kinds of resistance whenever we undertake a challenging endeavor. Starting a nonprofit is no exception. You will experience resistance at most every turn with only sporadic encouragement along the way.

Here are some of the challenges or types of resistance that you may encounter.

### EMOTIONAL CHALLENGES

You will likely feel a "high" associated with dreaming about your vision, receiving your incorporation papers and 501(c)(3) status, developing a logo, thinking about the generational impact of your vision...and so on. I know because I've experienced all of this. But soon you are confronted with the reality of the undertaking.

Astute businesspeople who are interested in investing in your mission ask difficult questions like: "What happens to your mission if something happens to you? How are you going to fund this in perpetuity? Who is on your board of directors? Who has donated significantly to you up to this point? Are you sure you can get zoning for what you want to do?" This is just an abbreviated list, and addressing questions like these can be emotionally exhausting.

### PHYSICAL CHALLENGES

I routinely worked about 14 hours a day for three years. I wasn't married and didn't have children, so I had the bandwidth to invest that kind of time. I freely admit that my drive exceeded my talent, but at that point in my life, all I knew was to grind it out. I lost almost 40 pounds, and I was so tired that some nights I couldn't sleep.

Although hard, focused work is essential, always be sensitive to not let your "drivenness" exceed your "calledness."

We are holistic beings called to live balanced lives, and rest is critical to that balance.

SEASON ONE: FOUNDING

*Always be sensitive to not let your drivenness exceed your calledness.*

### SOCIAL CHALLENGES

Many of your friendships can become connected to your mission through funding or an early governing body. It can become difficult to have a normal life and relationships outside of your mission "bubble."

### MENTAL CHALLENGES

Starting a nonprofit involves spinning a lot of plates at the same time. I am naturally a focused person, but trying to maintain that discipline with so many needs to address was very challenging.

Here are just a few things you will need to think about and execute: communications needs such as developing a website and collaterals; recruiting advocates for your mission, whether board members or those who are professionals in your space; raising funds to survive as the lone employee; undertaking the land search and negotiating terms for purchase; and finally, developing a well-thought-out business plan that captures the need, the vision to meet that need, and capital and operational financial pro formas. All of these tasks take concerted mental effort to execute well.

### SPIRITUAL RESISTANCE

You will always face spiritual resistance in the unseen realm that doesn't want your efforts to come to reality. To think otherwise is naive. The enemy has many ways to discourage, distract, and derail you in this critical journey to launch your mission. The spiritual antidote for this is supernatural dependence on God during this season.

### FAMILY CHALLENGES

When a founder feels called to a mission, their family must be called as well. I have personally witnessed a founder dragging his family to the mission field; the results were disastrous for both the ministry and the family. There can be so many casualties when family members are not aligned. This warning isn't only for those whose family accompanies them into a physical mission field. A founder always carries the weight and responsibility of the mission, many of which are listed in the aforementioned challenges.

My wife, Kayanne, met me when I had already been "on mission" for three years. While living on the Ranch after we married, she faithfully served our Ranch community, was an incredible encourager and support to me, all the while being a wonderful mother to our five children. I cannot imagine having a partner who did not fully embrace the mission to which God called me. Even with that, it was very hard.

I have also witnessed the incredible benefit when a family on mission sees firsthand God do what only He can do. It is edifying not only to the faith of individual family members but the corporate faith of the family. Anything can be accomplished if everybody is pulling in the same direction and believes they are pursuing something bigger than themselves.

The "weight" a founder carries can take away time from family life. But looking back over our time at the Ranch, the positives of my family living in a ministry setting far outweighed the downside. Eagle Ranch is very much a part of not just my legacy but also our family's legacy.

## KEY LESSON

It is helpful to know some of the key challenges and resistance you will face in advance and to prepare yourself for the long haul. Those early days were the hardest times of my life but at the same time the absolute best. I felt this incredible connectedness to God as we were on this ambitious and challenging journey together.

*How have you prepared yourself for the challenges you will face?*
*Is there alignment with your spouse and family on your "calling?"*

# Defining Your Mission

## First Things First—Identifying Your "Why"

Many times, in my consulting role with nonprofits, I'm asked to help develop or refine the organization's mission statement. First, I encourage them to step back and look at their *why*.

The "why" of your organization is the reason it exists. Understanding and developing your organizational why takes a good bit of introspection and soul searching to go beyond the superficial reasons for your organization's existence.

For instance, you may state that you exist to provide a home for children who struggle in life. But at a deeper level, what are the reasons this is so important to you? That is your why.

### HOW I FOUND MY WHY

To unearth my why, which manifested itself in the establishment of Eagle Ranch, I needed to look backward to deep heart resolves that shaped and motivated me in my earlier years.

One pivotal moment was my sophomore year at Auburn. In the evening, I would make the near-mile walk from my apartment to a small church that stayed open 24/7. I sat among empty pews struggling with my life's direction: Did I want to follow a logical path that aligned with my talents and gifts (at least how I perceived them)? Or did I want to abandon myself to God's power and His reason for putting me on this earth?

This latter route was really a test of my faith. If God wasn't who He said He was, I would have a pretty miserable life chasing a "ghost." Ultimately, I decided to go for broke and totally trust Him with my life's direction and purpose.

As the plans for Eagle Ranch began to take shape, God was clearly at the helm. Our staff, board and all those who have come alongside this mission have experienced "God at work" beyond their own giftedness or even their collective efforts. As a result, we can all testify that we have witnessed God's power in the beginnings and unfolding of Eagle Ranch.

This experience of God's work is the first part of Eagle Ranch's why: To be a tangible expression of God's goodness and power in this world.

SEASON ONE: FOUNDING

When people look at Eagle Ranch, I hope they see God operating in this world. We want them to look at Jesus and not an individual or group of individuals. This desire was foundational for me. I wanted to experience personally, and I wanted others to experience corporately, a God who is alive and well and doing great things on this earth.

The second part of our why is to be the hands and feet of Jesus to those who are struggling.

In my adolescent years, I was struck with how incredibly blessed I was to grow up in a stable, nurturing home and with the realization that it was only because of the grace of God. When I would see someone who was disadvantaged or hurting, it would greatly burden me and draw me into their story. It was as if this burden for those who struggle was embedded in the essence of who I am. I wasn't sure how this would manifest itself in my adult years—only that my life's path was probably going to be one of serving others.

It was out of gratitude for what God did for me that I wanted to help others who were less fortunate. I found it to be an incredible privilege to enter another person's story and provide hope and a vision for a better life, to communicate God's good plan for them, and be part of redirecting the course of their life. This was core to my motivation, to my why.

My encouragement to you is to spend time and think deeply about the why behind what you want to do.

> *Spend time and think deeply about the why behind what you want to do.*

Ultimately, that is what resonates most with your staff and donors. Many times, the "what, how and when" become white noise. Your why never does. It reaches people at a deeper level and motivates them to engage in your mission.

### KEY LESSON

Your why is your essence, your reason, and in challenging days, it becomes a place of encouragement, recalibration, and motivation to continue forward.

*When looking at your why, ask questions such as, "What is my essence?" and "What is my North Star?" That is far more important than what you do or how you do it. The answers to those questions flow naturally out of your why.*

## The Importance of Focus

One of my good friends and a valued mentor is one of the top pastors in America. When I asked him for the secret to his success, he said, "Focus, focus, focus." In my consulting, I have found that a primary reason new ventures fail is lack of focus.

Focus is embedded in every aspect of our mission: program services, communications, fundraising, physical plant development, and long-term planning. Because of its importance, focus is addressed throughout this book.

Pay special attention to developing a plan that is executable and consistent with your organization's maturity level. You can always expand and innovate beyond the original vision, but to start out with too broad a vision usually results in a mission never getting off the ground.

For instance, Eagle Ranch started as a boys' ranch. Fifteen years later, we added a girls' program and a SACS-accredited on-campus school. We were able to launch those two significant initiatives simultaneously because we were so focused. We were able to pivot off that cornerstone (boys' ranch) to incorporate these two initiatives both operationally and culturally. In subsequent years, we added equine therapy, more intentional work with families, and other initiatives. If we had launched these programs at our inception, it would have doomed Eagle Ranch.

Another value of focus is donor relations. Astute businesspeople understand that an unfocused undertaking is a recipe for disaster. One time I was asked to serve as a consultant for a large family foundation. The foundation was confused about someone's inner-city vision that was being presented for funding. As I sat through the presentation and listened to this individual communicate their vision, I was quite honestly lost.

SEASON ONE: FOUNDING

He wanted to accomplish so many things to accommodate so many different audiences that it left my head spinning. When he left an hour later, the foundation directors looked at me as if to ask, "Well?" I said, "I'm not quite sure what he is trying to do." Much to their relief, they said, "That's exactly how we felt." Needless to say, that individual did not receive funding from this foundation.

Ironically, the next day, someone asked me to meet with an individual who wanted to create clean water capacity for an East African village. The individual presented a succinctly focused plan that went something like this: "We need to drill a well in this area, a pump to draw the water out of the well, and a storage tank. The total cost is $40,000. The reason we need to do this is because there is no clean water within five miles of this village." End of presentation.

It was a stark contrast to the presentation I'd heard the day before, and it made me want to contribute to this focused, very strategic vision. The presenter didn't exhaust me with endless scenarios but rather a vision that was focused and made sense. His presentation gave me such energy that I felt compelled to ask what was next, and he was *ready* with an expanded vision. He said they wanted to use some of the water from the well to build a concrete block business. The necessary components of that project were a Butler building, some machinery, and an additional storage tank. The total cost was $60,000. I wanted to

*A primary reason new ventures fail is lack of focus.*

SEASON ONE: FOUNDING

give to that project, too. (Interestingly, this presentation was almost 20 years ago, and I still remember it!)

Stay focused on your vision; if people want to know more, they will ask. Be ready with plans beyond your focus area in case that question comes, but leading with a voluminous, unfocused proposal results in loss of credibility and opportunity.

> **KEY LESSON**
>
> Focused endeavors give you the margin and opportunity to pivot into other synergistic opportunities. If you can't succinctly describe your mission on one piece of paper, then you could have a focus issue. Bigger is not better.
>
> *Can you concisely describe the need and a focused strategy to meet that need?*

## Surrounding Yourself with Truth Tellers

I once shared with my wife some of the hard questions I ask when people come to me for counsel about the mission they want to pursue. She questioned my directness, pointing out how discouraging it could be to these well-meaning individuals.

My reply was that if people are called to a mission, hard feedback will not deter them from pursuing their dream. It is quite honestly a gift to challenge them to look deeper and ask themselves: Can I really do this? Do I really want to do this?

### THE GIFT OF REALITY

As you become more competent and known in your space, you will be sought out for advice; that was certainly true for me and Eagle Ranch. Initially, random individuals and organizations would contact me for counsel. My advice-giving later evolved to funneling those folks into seminars to share the principles and intricacies of starting a nonprofit positioned for excellence.

In the early days of these seminars, I would share three things that would dissuade 95 percent of the people in attendance from pursuing their nonprofit dream. First, your mission is a business, and if the business isn't run well, the clients you serve will suffer the consequences. Secondly, if you started full-time today, it will be two to three years—at the earliest—before your first clients arrive. And finally, because of this being a business, you as Executive Director will become less involved in direct mission work, increasingly losing one-on-one contact with your clients as you lead fundraising, communications, and program service development, among many other responsibilities.

As I look back on the 500 or so folks who came through our seminars, probably only 25 of those moved forward with their mission. At first, I was distraught at that percentage. But after I thought about it, I was encouraged that the 475 who didn't pursue their "dream" were able to move on with their lives. Some of them had held onto the vision of starting a children's home or other nonprofit since their childhood, and when the gift of reality was given to them, they were able to redirect their energy and allow space for what God actually planned for them in the future.

## RECRUITING TRUTH TELLERS

Truthfulness is a gift, and too many cheerleaders in your life can make you blind to the potential pitfalls or shortcomings of an undertaking. Truth tellers are needed to ask direct questions, challenge your plans, and hold you accountable.

When recruiting these early truth tellers, close friends and family members may not be the best choice, as they may struggle to communicate hard truths or hold you accountable. They can, however, connect you with more objective community and business leaders who might be a better fit.

I would caution you to keep a distinction between early truth tellers and your first board members. You may eventually ask some of these truth tellers to be on your board, but promising a place on the board too early could impact their objectivity.

> ### KEY LESSON
>
> Seek the hard questions and look for truth in the feedback you receive from your worst critics. Recruit objective truth tellers who aren't too close to you or your vision. If you make it through the "truth-telling gauntlet," you are ready to start laying the foundation for your organization.
>
> *How do you receive truth?*
> *Do you take it too personally?*
> *Who are some truth tellers in your life?*
> *What aspects of your plans would especially benefit from the truth-telling gauntlet?*

## Building and Engaging Your Board

An engaged and strategically-positioned board of directors will provide vibrant leadership for your mission.

As you recruit board members, look for people with different skillsets and broad expertise on all the processes that drive your mission: program services, human resources, communications, fundraising, and finance.

### MUTUAL TRUST

In the summer of 2000, almost 15 years after starting the Ranch, I experienced a significant burnout such that I needed to completely "unplug" from Eagle Ranch for three months. That meant no correspondence, phone calls or emails. At this point, our board of directors, specifically the executive committee, in concert with the Ranch's senior leadership team, took over the operations of our mission. If we had a board that was poorly positioned or one that didn't have ownership in our mission, I'm not sure how the Ranch would have fared during that critical time or even continued to exist.

The level of trust and respect between me as the founder and our board needed to be high to allow for this time away. In order to truly let go, I had to trust that the board would keep the mission moving in a positive direction. Conversely, the board needed to trust that I would take the time needed to "heal" without interfering with the Ranch operations so that I could come back refueled and ready to resume leadership.

Because we had already established strong trust, my time off and return to leadership were seamless.

### DON'T CREATE A RUBBER STAMP BOARD

In addition to mutual trust, a leader and board will at times face respectful tension. This tension is both necessary and beneficial to a healthy organization.

One of the greatest detriments to the mission of a nonprofit is commonly called a rubber stamp board. For instance, a charismatic, persuasive founder shares a vision without communicating both the positive and negative implications. As a result, the board ends up making ill-informed and not well-thought-out recommendations. It takes self-discipline for a leader to present both sides of the equation, especially when they are passionate about a particular direction. But the board also has the responsibility to ask probing questions, especially as it pertains to strategic initiatives.

In 2018, I was tasked by our board to present the plan for creation of what is now known as The Wings Center. Architectural drawings, capital and operational pro formas, and projected personnel growth were just a few of the items required for my report to the board. I felt that I had "crossed every t and dotted every i" until my presentation at our annual board retreat. What had started out as a perfunctory board report (or so I thought) became a vigorous question-and-answer session that resulted in The Wings Center being postponed for nearly a year until more comprehensive work was done.

Initially, I was taken aback by their decision. After all, I was an experienced leader and historically had been very conservative in expanding the Ranch mission.

In retrospect, they were absolutely right. After two years of operations, we met or exceeded all recalibrated assumptions of The Wings Center's operations.

Sometimes it's hard to believe that the board is "for" you when they push back, but it's far more important that they are for the mission. The mission is bigger than one person or one board member, so be very prayerful and strategic about board selections.

As my time as executive director was coming to a close, I would physically leave the boardroom at the end of board meetings. This enabled the board to engage in confidential conversations, and it also served as a subtle reminder that this was the board's mission as much as it had ever been mine. I can honestly say that throughout my tenure as executive director, our board has truly executed their role as guardians of our mission with the utmost integrity.

### ENGAGING YOUR BOARD

Every nonprofit with whom I have consulted has asked for help with their board of directors. These are just a few of their concerns:

*"I have too many inactive board members."*
*"I have board members who are not aligned with our mission."*

*It's hard to believe that the board is for you when they push back, but it's far more important that they are for the mission.*

SEASON ONE: FOUNDING

*"We don't have a system for rotating board members on and off the board."*
*"It's difficult to get quality board members."*
*"The board doesn't ask hard questions of the executive director."*

In response to these issues and others, here are some high-level points to reflect on:

First, consider not only skillsets when recruiting a board member, but also assess the cultural fit. An organization I recently consulted with had to "fire" a Type-A board member who had a disruptive "over-ownership" of the mission and no appreciation of the collaborative ethos of the board.

Another consideration is whether a board member is agenda driven outside the core mission of the organization. This can take the form of religious, social or even political agendas. I have seen this to be a major distraction to an organization's focused mission.

A board member orientation is crucial for helping new board members bring value early on in their board tenure. In the early days of the Ranch, the orientation process was largely perfunctory, but now it has evolved into an almost daylong exposure to Eagle Ranch. Even after agreeing to serve on the board, people had no idea of the scale and complexity of the Ranch. This orientation gave them a fresh understanding and perspective on how they could be contributing members of the board from Day One.

Our orientation process is very detailed and strategic, as new board members meet with multiple members of our senior and front-line staff to get a high level and behind-the-scenes perspective on the Ranch's operations. This is also a great early barometer of a prospective board member's commitment level. If they can't give you a day to learn about the organization, then they probably are not going to be committed to your quarterly board meetings.

Finally, you must keep board members engaged. A number of factors can affect the commitment level of your board members, including: the board is too large (I won't be missed), board attendance isn't taken seriously (this can be contagious), board members are not asked for their input (they just get reported to), they have too many other commitments (you want busy people, but...); and there is nothing going on with the mission or in the board meeting that invigorates them (the executive director's responsibility is to provide educational, inquisitive, and inspiring meetings).

How can you remedy these challenges? Some ideas to facilitate engagement are:

- Host "Lunch and Learns" at board meetings on different aspects of the mission.

SEASON ONE: FOUNDING

- Ensure the timely distribution of board minutes after the meetings.

- Send notes of appreciation to board members for their individual contributions at board meetings.

- Make a phone call to each board member the day after board meetings to reinforce their contributions—even if you have to leave a voicemail.

- Schedule periodic one-on-one meetings with board members over the course of the year.

- Ensure that the board is not just "reported to"; encourage discussion.

- Use closed sessions for confidential and thought-provoking discussions.

- Schedule an annual one-day off-site retreat to encourage relationship building and vision casting.

- Respect term limits. It gives board members an opportunity to be celebrated for their years of service. They can always rotate back on the board at a later date for their respective talents and institutional knowledge.

## KEY LESSON

Recruit board members who have essential skillsets, are good cultural fits, and who ask the hard questions; curiosity is an asset. Engage board members through continuing education, asking for their feedback, encouraging discussion, and regularly touching base outside of board meetings.

*What board member skills would be especially beneficial at this stage of your organizational growth?*
*What are some ways to get your board members to be more engaged?*

TAKE A DEEPER DIVE ON HOW TO EFFECTIVELY BUILD AND OPERATE A BOARD OF DIRECTORS.

SEASON ONE: FOUNDING

# A Firm Foundation

"Not every organization is meant to outlive its founder." I spoke those words to an iconic ministry in Kentucky whose 70-year-old founder was preparing to step aside. His vibrant ministry touched the lives of hundreds of children and adolescents.

When I said this to him and his board, you could have heard a pin drop. They were shocked. Could my words possibly be true? Had this ministry seen its best days and was now destined to slowly fade into the sunset?

In his book *Built to Last*, Jim Collins' overarching premise is that companies that thrive in the future are built on a strong foundation and are positioned for sustainability.

When an organization begins, a fundamental question is: Do we want this organization to continue, or is it a founder-inspired and founder-expired organization? This is an important question because specific organizational strategies will evolve depending on which scenario is chosen.

Regardless of the vision for sustainability, building a strong foundation is crucial to a successful organization. I have consistently found that it takes about two to three years of foundational work prior to beginning operations. Some of this work involves:

• Creating policies and procedures

- Establishing transparent and disciplined accounting practices

- Positioning communications (if you miss this on the front end, you will pay for it many years later)

- Developing collaborative relationships within the community

- Identifying initial staffing needs and creating an initial organizational chart

- Outlining fundraising strategies

- Considering facility and physical plant needs

- Engaging in board development

**EARLY STAGES OF THE ORGANIZATION**

An executive director of a nonprofit in the Midwest was offered a significant amount of money to jumpstart his ministry just one year after launching. We had several long discussions about whether he should accept the money since it was predicated on beginning several new projects immediately. The choice came down to moving ahead with construction while navigating the missional foundational work or turning down significant funds in hopes that the donors would still be there later.

He accepted the money and began the new projects as the organization was still in its development stage. This decision led to some very difficult years that actually compromised the ministry's near-term ability to grow.

Conversely, by God's grace, at Eagle Ranch we didn't have that temptation and were able to stay focused on our three years of foundational work. As a result, once that foundation was laid, we built four children's homes in four consecutive years. Completing the foundational work enables faster growth, sets the stage for sustainability, and fosters innovation.

## AN ORGANIZATION FOR THE FUTURE

The organizational paradigm becomes more complex when sustainability is a goal. You have to have great discipline to develop an organization that respects the founder's giftedness but also has a sensitivity toward a future without that person in the CEO role.

For the retiring founder in Kentucky, the answer to his dilemma was found when a young man who had benefitted greatly from this organization expressed interest in stepping into the executive director's role. I believe this organization continues to this day, albeit in a slightly different paradigm. A sustainable organization does not necessarily need to mirror the original organization, which is

*Completing the foundational work enables faster growth, sets the stage for sustainability, and fosters innovation.*

often skewed to a founder's unique personality.

You may have a dynamic and talented founder who raises significant funds and becomes the organizational "brand." This is a big mistake. They are one heartbeat away from not being in that leadership role, and the organization will dissipate like a mist. Organizations that are built to last develop their own brand separate from, but in concert with the founder.

### RUN THE BUSINESS WELL

Leaders often face a temptation to neglect parts of an organization because one area is particularly effective. As a result, you can become complacent as you project one facet's excellence on the rest of an underdeveloped organization.

I had a good friend in the Northeast well-known in his nonprofit space. He was an incredibly gifted speaker and visionary. By his own admission, administration and management were not in his gift mix.

When it was time for his leadership transition, his desire was to turn over the reins to someone who would continue this impactful ministry in its current state. Unfortunately, some aspects of this ministry were reflections of my friend's force of personality and entrepreneurialism, and as it turns out, something that his successor could not execute.

Saddling a successor with a vision that is so tied to a founder's personality and giftedness is a recipe for disaster. Needless to say, this first successor didn't last, nor did the next one. They tried (and failed) to execute a ministry that wasn't replicable in its original state.

In this organization's case, they needed to spin off divisions of the ministry that were not core or sustainable. The great news is that the core business led by a gifted successor (its third) is thriving today, but it took a realistic look at the organization to decide what was sustainable and what was not.

### KEY LESSON

While it is exciting to gain momentum in the early days of your ministry, don't shortcut the foundational work. Determine your strategy for sustainability and position the organization accordingly from the start.

*Do you believe your ministry needs to outlive your tenure? If so, what needs to be put in place to ensure that it is possible? To what degree is the organization's brand and identity independent of yours or that of the founder?*

SEASON ONE: FOUNDING

## Learning from Others

I can honestly say there is not a children's program or nonprofit in this country that doesn't do something better than we do. When I visit other programs, I have a standard list of questions, but my goal is to bring back one or two nuggets to Eagle Ranch to make us better. This practice is especially beneficial in the early years of operation. I did this annually for over 10 years, even when these trips were financially difficult.

Seeing how other organizations operate gives you valuable perspective—both encouraging and challenging. It confirms the many things that you are doing well and may have previously taken for granted. You are also confronted with opportunities for improvement. Most of our new initiatives were born out of visiting other homes and seeing things in a new and different way.

In our travels, some visits provided a "warning shot" about the potential perils of a particular programmatic direction. For instance, we learned the challenges of having an independent living home or emergency shelter on our residential campus as opposed to off-campus.

Another problematic scenario was where a nonprofit founder's high profile and strong personality dwarfed the organization he was leading. Will this organization survive the founder's departure?

It also becomes oddly comforting that others experience

the same kind of challenges that you are facing, so you don't feel quite so alone in a challenging field.

These visits are especially important when developing your mission so you can build relationships and confirm you are not duplicating services in a particular area. There is nothing worse than coming into an area acting as if you will save that community from the maladies that have existed for many years. That's a quick way to ostracize yourself from others in the caregiving community, not just those in your specific space.

Learn where your mission fits within a community's spectrum of services. Ideally, that place is complementary or supplementary if there is a legitimate unmet need.

When we built The Wings Center, we wanted to be a partner to help address the mental health crisis in our area and beyond through outpatient counseling. We cited that so many people are already doing good work. We wanted to be part of that good work in the process of building collaborative efforts in helping children, families, and individuals live emotionally healthy lives.

We strove to cultivate or even safeguard the mindset that we are "all on the same team" wanting the same things. Being territorial can become increasingly problematic in so many ways. As Robert Woodruff, former CEO and Chairman of The Coca-Cola Company, once said, "There is no limit to what a man can do or where he can go if he doesn't mind who gets the credit."

SEASON ONE: FOUNDING

As your mission matures, remember this key lesson I learned from visiting other organizations in both the for-profit and nonprofit space: the timeless admonition that "bigger is not necessarily better." Always keep in mind the future implications of changing even one person's life.

Positioning your mission effectively, regardless of size, will have great impact—one life at a time.

### KEY LESSON

Continue to refine your mission by visiting similar organizations in your nonprofit space. As you learn from others, be willing to share lessons from your journey. Your organization will likely be part of a community that has other caregivers with similar or complementary goals. Build relationships and establish your mission within the collaborative fabric of the community.

*Can you identify organizations within and outside your community that may have important lessons for you?*
*When did you last purposefully visit a similar organization to learn and gather ideas?*

SEASON TWO

# Leading

## *Leading Thoughts*

BEFORE you can lead others, you must first be willing to lead yourself. When I look back over my four-decade tenure at Eagle Ranch, one of my biggest regrets is that my "drivenness exceeded my calledness." I've always valued a strong work ethic, but many times, grinding it out left me depleted spiritually, emotionally and physically. I share this because if left unchecked this is where most founders find themselves. No one is immune.

Fifteen years after starting Eagle Ranch, I began having challenges that I wasn't used to: memory issues, lack of focus, and worsening physical symptoms (inability to sleep, shaking, constant exhaustion). My doctor confirmed that I was experiencing post-adrenaline exhaustion. He bluntly stated that I needed an extended period of time away (three months) from my Ranch responsibilities to rest. No medication was prescribed, just rest.

That news was both discouraging and encouraging. I knew something was wrong. I just didn't know how to fix it.

I wish I had the wisdom in those early days to recognize this destructive pattern. It cost me, my staff and, most importantly, my family. If you are not self-aware, your mind and body will begin to communicate that all is not well.

The time away was difficult but needed. It was important for me to realize that if I came back to Eagle Ranch and repeated the same unhealthy pattern, I would be back in the same position a year later.

After three months, I felt completely restored. I never went back down that destructive road again, but I had to take an honest and sobering look at why I got there in the first place.

I learned to develop a new life rhythm: a more reasonable work/life balance, daily exercise, and finally, taking one day a month to go away to reflect and pray. That monthly day away has had the most profound impact, as it helps me to continually reflect on God's goodness and provision in my life and on my priorities.

One of my first meetings after arriving in Georgia was with a well-respected ministry leader. He told me simply, "Eddie, before you can take care of others, you need to first take care of yourself. We are most effective when we serve out of an overflow, not a deficit."

How true those words were then and continue to be for me.

# Launching Your Mission

### Building Your Team

In developing an organization, one of the most gratifying milestones is when you are ready to build your team. Those early individuals, whether staff or board members, need to align with your vision. They will set the tone for future generations joining your mission.

As you build your team, consider factors like these: alignment with your why, a sense of calling, commitment to excellence and professionalism, humility, and a willingness to grow personally.

Excellence and professionalism are especially important to establish from the start. You only get one chance to make a first impression, and if your early hires don't reflect how you want to be perceived both internally and externally, it will take many years (if ever) to correct that impression.

My initial staff—Jean Parks (executive administrator), Bruce Burch (counselor), and Tony and Trish Dittmeier (houseparents)—personified so much of what we desired in future hirings.

Another quality I look for as I recruit people is at least some for-profit experience because that often means an increased rigor of expectations.

People tend to gravitate to a ministry like Eagle Ranch for one of three reasons: those with a calling by God to serve, wanting to do societal good, or those dealing with significant emotional needs themselves. We only want to hire those in the first category. Empowerment by the Holy Spirit is crucial to us doing the spiritual work of Eagle Ranch. The Ranch would not be where it is today if we continually relied on our own human strength, experience, and wisdom.

## CONFRONT QUICKLY, HIRE SLOWLY

Excellent books have been written on hiring strategies, so I don't want to go into many of those here, but one thing that is particularly instructive for the nonprofit sector is to confront quickly and hire slowly.

What does this mean? I have seen numerous organizations unwilling to make a change and the mission

SEASON TWO: LEADING

suffered because of the lack of courage by the leader to make a difficult call. Nonprofit leaders can be overly gracious in their hiring and termination practices, but this is one of the areas where behaving more like a for-profit organization can be beneficial.

I have had to make very difficult decisions over the years with some long-time employees of the Ranch. Although they had served faithfully and were valued members of our Ranch family, it had become increasingly clear that the organization had outgrown their individual giftedness. In our conversations, I thanked them for their years of service and shared that we were going to move in a different direction with their position. Initially, this was met with anger, but years later, most reached out and said God used this decision to move them into a new season, and as a result, they were experiencing some of the best years of their lives.

Necessarily, early hires tend to be more generalists, then as the organization matures you will bring on more niche players or specialists. This will necessitate hard calls about people who don't have the specialized training needed in a more mature organization. Sometimes it is impossible to reposition those folks within the organization and there needs to be a parting of ways. This can be very difficult because they may have been very loyal co-laborers, especially in those early days of the organization. It ultimately comes down to a stewardship issue—both of their lives and the organization—and your willingness to make that difficult call.

**FINE-TUNING THE PROCESS**

Another hiring strategy we have developed is to continually fine-tune what we are looking for—and *not* looking for—especially as it pertains to those who interact directly with our children. For instance, we look at the personality and emotional profiles of houseparents who have done well and those couples who were not as effective. This is not an exact science, but it can keep you in the guardrails regarding who has a good chance of being effective in a particular role.

It may seem counterintuitive, but we rarely hire a houseparent couple from a similar mission space, because they come to us with expectations—both good and bad—that they can project on to Eagle Ranch. We prefer couples to come with a clean slate, so we can teach them our unique approach to serving children and families.

I love what Eagle Ranch advisor Dr. Tim Irwin said in his book *Impact: Great Leadership Changes Everything*: "You can find competent people, but are those people culturally a good fit?" This is where a hire rises or falls. Will the prospective employee be effective within a culturally-sensitive organization? If they don't fit culturally, their competence doesn't make any difference. They will be a drain on the mission, damage the culture and eventually

SEASON TWO: LEADING

*If they don't fit culturally, their competence doesn't make any difference.*

become isolated, and burn-out.

A lot of pain can be avoided by doing thoughtful, detailed work up front. Prepare your interview questions carefully in advance. Don't forget to finish with a complete reference check. Candidate-supplied references are usually positively biased. Try to find individuals whose names surfaced from sources other than the candidate who can give you unfiltered feedback. I'm always surprised by the number of organizations that don't check references or get an outside expert to interview and test the candidate.

Great candidate interviewing is an art. We ask behavioral interview questions using past indicators to demonstrate the presence or absence of the skills and aptitudes we need in our organization. Look for evidence that the candidate has been successful in doing exactly what you need done. For instance, what leadership traits has the candidate demonstrated? You might ask, "How have you grown a mature and collaborative leadership team? How do you encourage your team to perform at a high level? How do you approach conflict or tension in your team?" The specificity and quality of their examples can give good insight into how a person will live out their role in our organization. The greatest indicator of future performance is past performance.

Additionally, one of the best screens is an interviewee's social media activity. It is often a realistic glimpse

SEASON TWO: LEADING

into a person's interests and personality. I've interviewed several candidates in the final stages of our process only to find them to be very active and vocal in their political beliefs. People with agendas other than your core mission can be a significant cultural distraction.

## NO SHORTCUTS

You may be tempted to take shortcuts on hirings, especially when you have a vacancy for a crucial role. While not filling a role quickly may present organizational challenges, filling it prematurely can result in long-term problems for the organization.

Not giving into hiring shortcuts builds organizational resiliency and processes. You will have numerous opportunities to take matters into your own hands, to make something happen prematurely rather than depending on God. In the long term, that can compromise your mission.

In the interim, staff members sharing duties and selflessly serving the mission can build community and organizational capacity.

> ### KEY LESSON
>
> Hiring is a critical process in the growth of an organization. The quality of your hires will reflect your mission both internally and externally. Take your time when hiring and don't hold onto people who have become ineffective or misaligned as your organization matures.
>
> *What are interview questions that will provide key insight into an individual's fit in your organization?*
> *Are there people who are currently on your staff you would not hire again because of competency issues or who are not a cultural fit? What is your next step with them?*

## Sharing Your Story

When I share Eagle Ranch's why, I find myself communicating passionately. I feel like I am reaching into another person's heart and asking, "Can you see the value of what's being accomplished here? Don't you want to get involved?" These are questions that I don't necessarily verbalize but feel in my heart.

SEASON TWO: LEADING

**THE POWER OF STORYTELLING**

Jesus told stories because there is something about communicating anecdotally that moves people to action. Your storytelling needs to be rooted in your why—the genesis of the vision. Before a mission statement or vision statement is established, the founder needs to understand at a very deep level the why behind their organization. The fact I've mentioned this several times before underscores its importance.

Storytelling is in stark contrast to communication focused on what, how, and when. As shared earlier, your why is at your very core, your essence. "Living the Vision of God," Dallas Willard's article, speaks about the fire of a founder that fuels their passion for the mission. I want to bring people to the fire itself, not just the "effects" of the fire (i.e., reputation, programs, facilities, finances, systems, processes). Many people tend to only communicate the lukewarm effects of the fire instead of communicating the burning coals to an audience.

**WHO, HOW AND WHY**

In addition to positioning your why at the core of your communications, it's important to express how it manifests itself. In other words, who do you want to reach (children and families), how do you want to reach them (holistically), and why is it important (generations will have a better life). Communicating these manifestations

*Your storytelling needs to be rooted in your why— the genesis of the vision.*

through illustrations makes your why come alive.

In your storytelling, speak about struggling people in such a way that if they were in the audience, they would not be embarrassed. In the early days of Eagle Ranch, I cringed at the very thought of one of our Ranch children being in attendance. Thankfully, I became convicted that sharing too much could be viewed as exploitive and, as a result, became much more careful with my words.

Since then, I have given talks when some of our Ranch children or parents have been in an audience, and afterward they commented with appreciation on how they were portrayed. Social nonprofits are infamous for exploiting their clients even though it's usually done anonymously. Be careful here. It's always helpful to picture someone you serve being in the audience. How would you feel if that person were you?

A great question to ask yourself and your audience: If your organization never existed, what would be the implications for your community and beyond? I mentioned that question ("What if Eagle Ranch never existed?") at a large event once, and there was silence as people thought through the implications of that question.

### TRANSPARENCY

Don't communicate misleading information to gain donor approval. A perceptive and strategic donor will drill down for specifics, and you will lose credibility. It's best to be forthcoming about struggles and challenges—that's the real world. I have found most donors to be very empathetic.

One of our most effective newsletters in the early days of the Ranch was when I described a child who was not a success story and continued to struggle in his life. I was really convicted that his story needed to be shared but was worried about how it would be perceived by our donors. Would they question our competency or rethink their support? Yet I was convinced that our donors needed to see the "other side of the coin." We wanted to communicate not just the good fruit of our labor but also acknowledge those situations that, at least in the near term, looked dire. What an overwhelming response we received from that newsletter as several commented in follow-up letters about how refreshing this transparency was to them.

Positioning your organization continually as without fault or struggles does not enlist engagement in the long run.

A focused, succinct message (you never have to apologize for brevity) with storytelling is most effective in communicating your mission. For every major point you communicate, try to have a story illustration. Otherwise, your talk can come off as just dispensing information (white noise) to your audience.

SEASON TWO: LEADING

> ### KEY LESSON
>
> No one can tell your story better than you. Stories rooted in your why make your communication memorable and inspire people to act. Your stories should be authentic without misleading the audience or exploiting the struggles of those you serve.
>
> *How can you share your story in such a way that it compels people to action?*

VIEW BEST PRACTICES SURROUNDING MARKETING AND COMMUNICATIONS.

## Funding the Mission

In the early days of Eagle Ranch, we would receive about 10 pieces of mail a day, most of it junk mail. On one particular day, we received only two pieces of mail, which was very unusual for us. The first envelope was a check for $2.00—the smallest check we had ever received. The second envelope contained a check for $100,000—by far our largest gift in those early days. It was as if God were sending us a message: Love the giver, not the gift.

## A DISCIPLINED APPROACH

The people I consult with inevitably ask for the "silver bullet" behind Eagle Ranch's decades of strong financial health. In truth, there isn't one. It's just an adherence to strategic practices that over time have a high return on investment.

These practices are in the context of a commitment to do the hard work—day in and day out—with no ill-advised shortcuts. I have known many who have gone down that "compromising road." Although they may have some immediate success, in the long run compromises will spread in such a way that the organization drifts into unprincipled territory.

## WHY PEOPLE GIVE

We have learned that people give for three primary reasons: need, vision, and relationship.

The need must be documented by reliable third-party sources rather than just an anecdotal expression of the need.

The vision addresses how that need will be met. The vision should be focused (the simpler, the better) and make sense to a donor. An internal litmus test we use when determining whether to proceed with a vision or project is

SEASON TWO: LEADING

*People give for three primary reasons: need, vision, and relationship.*

the strength of the request narrative. If the narrative is "weak," it raises the question: Is there really a need? It will be difficult to enlist a potential donor in that project and could even compromise their future involvement.

Finally, relationships are crucial. Be careful about meeting with prospective donors through cold calling. It's wonderful if a donor initiates a meeting, but most of the time they do not. Your relationship with board members or others associated with your mission can provide valuable inroads to potential supporters. They have the most credibility in the community and with potential funders.

In the early 1980s, I asked Vince Dooley to introduce me to Rankin Smith, who at the time was the owner of the Atlanta Falcons, and Fran Tarkenton, a Hall of Fame NFL quarterback. There was a pause on the other end of the phone, as Coach Dooley was probably thinking, "Oh, really? Anything else?" Because of their relationship with Vince Dooley, both of these men were willing to meet with me. Both of them ended up supporting the Ranch.

Strategically building your board of directors can provide added influence and credibility across a broad spectrum. You certainly want to bring folks onto your board who have the necessary expertise, but their breadth of influence is almost equally as important. We call this "leveraging other's halos."

## THE BOARD AND GIVING

One of the questions I am most often asked is, "Do you require your board members to give to your organization?" The short answer is, "No." This is primarily for two reasons. First, if someone is not supporting the mission financially, it doesn't mean that they're not contributing in other ways. For instance, they may be supporting the organization through their talent and expertise or other types of volunteerism. Secondly, if they are not giving, it could be that the organizational leader isn't casting a compelling vision. It's easy to require board members to support your mission, but I think there are deeper issues that need to be considered. People's treasures will always follow their hearts.

One exception is if a prospective donor requires that all board members are financial supporters of your organization. In this instance, you can ask board members to make at least a small contribution to help meet this requirement.

## FOUNDER AS FUNDRAISER

At Eagle Ranch, we didn't hire a Director of Development until almost 20 years after we began our mission. This decision comes as a surprise to many.

I encourage a founder (at least initially) to take on the mantle as the organization's lead fundraiser. Because the organizational vision is embedded in their being, they can communicate the purpose and passion to a donor better than anyone. More than once, I have seen a founder offload this responsibility to a development officer, who perhaps is gifted in asking for support but will never be as close as the founder to the fire behind the vision. Eventually, you will likely have a need for a strong director of development. But even then, when there is a major financial opportunity, they will become "table setters" for the executive director.

When I came to Georgia, I raised funds begrudgingly. As an introvert, I didn't feel particularly comfortable asking for money. Thankfully, I learned that many times you don't have to ask but just be ready to respond to a donor's inquiry about the needs of your mission.

George Mueller, the founder of the Ashley Down Orphanage in England, is one of my heroes who inspired me in my founding days. He famously stated that he never asked for money during his time of seeing God's miraculous provision for his orphanage in Bristol, England. Rarely do people mention that George Mueller wrote about 70 handwritten thank-you notes a day. In some ways, that has become my model: to make sure that people are thanked quickly and consistently, and not treated like an ATM machine.

Eagle Ranch could not exist apart from God's provision, but it would be presumptive to believe we don't have a role in this provision. St. Augustine once said, "Pray as

SEASON TWO: LEADING

though everything depended on God. Work as if everything depended on you."

> ### KEY LESSON
>
> No one is likely better than the founder to articulate vision and motivate people to give. Never compromise for the sake of easy funding. One of the most impactful means of communicating is the handwritten note.
>
> *Do you believe that you are the chief fundraiser for your mission?*
> *Do you know how to effectively state your need to inspire giving?*

LEARN MORE ABOUT FUNDRAISING BEST PRACTICES.

LEARN MORE ABOUT BUILDING AN ENDOWMENT.

# Living a Mission-Led Culture

## Developing Your Culture

You've likely heard this many times: an organization is only as good as its people. Organizational culture is created and nurtured by a mix of intentional practices and what organically emerges.

A healthy culture is an accelerator of productivity. Conversely, when the culture is exposed to unpredictable, potentially volatile situations, it can set back a mission's progress. A culture not attended to moves toward chaos and disunity. Therefore, thoughtful strategies and accountability to protect your culture are crucial. It starts with building community.

I love what Dietrich Bonhoeffer said about community in his book *Life Together: The Classic Exploration of Christians in Community*. "The person who's in love with their vision of community will destroy community. But the person who loves the people around them will create community everywhere they go."

We can fall in love with the "idea" of community, but in the process fail to embrace the actual people who make up that community.

People who work at Eagle Ranch almost universally comment on how much they love living in the Ranch community. As a program that includes residential care, we have staff who live on our campus, so community extends beyond the workday into their daily lives.

One of the criteria we look for, especially with direct care staff, is whether they were previously involved in community activities such as a small group, community association, or civic club. Loners tend to struggle, as they can become isolated, especially during difficult times.

## CREATING A HEALTHY COMMUNITY

A healthy community is foundational for a healthy culture, and some people are naturally gifted in this area. As a natural introvert, I benefited from wonderful community builders on our staff, including our first counselor, Bruce Burch, who set the tone for the Eagle

## SEASON TWO: LEADING

Ranch culture in our earliest days.

Our community has been healthiest when we act from the Biblical mindset of sacrificially serving each other and thinking the best of each other. We emphasize the need to not rush to judgment or create false narratives about what we feel another person *may* think or say about us. We follow the Matthew 18:15 principle of discussing any differences face to face.

How someone lives in community can be a barometer as to whether they should continue with an organization. Increasing negativity is a telltale sign that a staff member's time could be nearing an end. When we operate continually out of a deficit as opposed to an overflow, negativity tends to be the result. A tired culture usually becomes an unhealthy culture. Developing creative strategies to keep staff members healthy will position them to serve out of an overflow.

One way we encourage our Ranch community is to empower them to see the impact they have on others outside the ministry. Proverbs 11:25 states, *"...Whoever refreshes others are themselves refreshed."* We go beyond the borders of our staff community to serve others so we don't become too inward focused. To this end, the Ranch hosts annual events to encourage, educate, and train others in surrounding communities. In conjunction with the Ranch children, we serve our community—the elderly, food banks, and relief efforts, just to name a few.

A closed "circle the wagons" mentality can lead to a sense of entitlement that evolves into a siloed organization where people become territorial. This tendency can damage the health of the community and create lasting negative effects on the culture and the mission.

### ESTABLISHING ACCOUNTABILITY

At its core, accountability is really about growth. All of us are walking wounded; we all have blind spots. As the early church fathers used to say, it's a "severe mercy" to confront people when they stray.

Not only is it important to recognize positive behavior that is edifying to the organization in real-time, but also to quickly and courageously call out behavior that is inconsistent with core values. Failure to do so can severely compromise a culture.

Furthermore, as we correct the children we serve at Eagle Ranch and encourage them to grow in uncomfortable ways, we must be willing to do the same thing ourselves. It's easy for someone with power and authority to say that growth is for "them" and not for "us." Humility in this area produces a culture that is *growing together* into Christlikeness.

SEASON TWO: LEADING

> ### KEY LESSON
>
> Although culture is not quantifiable, the result of a healthy culture certainly is. Lay the groundwork to attract talented staff members who align with your why, value community and are willing to personally grow.
>
> *What is your vision to create a healthy community and culture?*
> *What are the essential attributes you desire in your staff?*

## Investing In Your Culture

Ongoing investment in the culture you have worked so hard to build is paramount for its continued success. Always remember that culture is never stagnant; it changes and is influenced as your community grows or experiences turnover.

There is always a danger that your why, mission statement, and the core values of your organization become nothing more than words on paper. So, to combat this, Eagle Ranch celebrates the real-time execution of our core values throughout the year. They truly are the guardrails of the mission enabling us to look forward with confidence to the future.

I remember speaking with Dan Cathy, who succeeded his father, Truett Cathy, as CEO of Chick-fil-A. Truett was the founder and loved the why behind Chick-fil-A. I asked Dan about his strategy to continue keeping the why of Chick-fil-A prominent with their employees. He mentioned that every new employee goes through a vision and values program spanning several days. Starting with their first restaurant in Hapeville, it traces the history, passion, and purpose of Chick-fil-A. To emphasize the importance of Chick-fil-A's desire to pass along its values, Dan Cathy personally led this initiative.

As a result, we developed our own Vision and Values day. At Eagle Ranch we have a mandatory meeting every year of all our staff to talk about our why and the core values flowing out of it. Your why requires special attention and must be consistently communicated to all levels of the organization. The author Samuel Johnson once said, "People need to be reminded more than instructed." Remind them what they already know.

### CARE FOR STAFF NEEDS

Another key in fostering a healthy culture is to nurture your staff's emotional and physical needs. You should provide reasonable time off, rest, and possibly sabbaticals to create ongoing margin in your employees' lives for their own well-being and for their families.

Those in the "people caring" space carry a lot of other people's trauma. They need a safe place to offload the burden they feel day in and day out. As a result, we provide counseling (usually off-site) to keep our frontline staff emotionally healthy. At the end of the day, emotionally-healthy people will be much more effective in serving their clients. It is worth the investment.

As a Christian organization, we want to continually remind our folks that this is a spiritual work and requires continued reliance on God's provision and protection. Therefore, we offer a weekly chapel service where we all come together for a time of prayer, devotion, and communion. These chapel times can sometimes seem inconvenient with demanding workloads and schedules, but it is an ongoing discipline declaring that this time set aside from work is worth it. Often it helps us recalibrate why we are doing what we are doing and our need for God to execute this mission.

**PROVIDE APPROPRIATE COMPENSATION**
In the 1980s, several scandals in the Christian nonprofit world revealed that some leaders were paying themselves exorbitant salaries. The abuse had become so extreme that some nonprofit executives went to prison. That was the backdrop when I arrived in Georgia to start the Ranch. I was single and didn't need a lot of money to

survive, so my first annual salary in 1982 was less than $10,000. I took pride in wanting to start Eagle Ranch for the right reasons and not to benefit financially.

Then one day, I was challenged by a peer who asked, "If you artificially reduce your salary, how does that impact those who work for you?" Just as artificially-inflated salaries can be damaging for an organization, so can artificially-deflated salaries.

You create a false economy as it pertains to what is needed to run your organization in a financially sustainable way. I have seen organizations wanting to experience the exhilaration of growth without having sufficient staff or paying current staff (including the executive director) appropriately.

Soon after my peer challenged me, we hired a compensation firm with access to the financial data of nonprofit organizations of every staff and budget size (with industry salary averages in our region of the country). Since then, we have stayed in the median range in our nonprofit space. Of course, salary levels shouldn't be so high that compensation becomes the main motivation for people wanting to work with you.

### ENCOURAGE AND CELEBRATE LONGEVITY

Finally, a healthy culture expects and celebrates longevity. At Eagle Ranch, I was in the executive director position for almost 40 years. Our initial counselor stayed

SEASON TWO: LEADING

35 years, and our executive administrator was with us for 36 years—many more staff members have stayed 10 or more years.

You certainly don't want people to stay past their effectiveness, but the real danger in many nonprofit organizations is people feeling "used" and not appreciated. The result is short tenures. We are constantly striving to create an environment where people want to co-labor in our mission for extended periods of time.

I am often asked how to create an environment for longer tenures. For us, I have found three main factors. First, is the strength of the call. As our first houseparents, Tony and Trish Dittmeier, once told me during a particularly difficult time, "Eddie, God called us to be here, and circumstances aren't going to call us away." The second factor is support. You don't want people to feel that they are alone on an island but rather are part of a team that is executing a very difficult mission. And finally, training. You want to provide people the tools and the knowledge to be effective with your clients. In my time at the Ranch, I have found that when all three of these areas align people feel engaged and empowered—and they stay.

## KEY LESSON

Continually invest in your culture by means of regularly reviewing the vision, mission and core values of your organization with your staff. Take extra care to develop ways to train, support, and appreciate your staff.

*How do you envision investing in your culture? What values do you want to be evident in your organization's culture?*

# Maintaining and Growing Your Mission

## Innovation

**INNOVATION AND TRADITION**

Leaders in the nonprofit space should hold both tradition and innovation lightly. I often see people over-romanticizing the past or minimizing it, but creating a balance is important. Eagle Ranch would be much less than it is today if we had not had a willingness to step into the future with strategic boldness.

We started out as a boys' ranch. If we had stopped there, we would have five boys' homes, eight boys per home, and that would have been the extent of Eagle

Ranch's mission. But today we have added a girls' program, an on-campus school, equine therapy, more intentional work with families, and The Wings Center.

As executive director, my successor, John Shackelford, and I have discussed the value of respecting Eagle Ranch's rich history as well as the need to continually innovate. I shudder to think what Eagle Ranch would be today if we failed to innovate during our four decades and had a death grip on "the way we've always done things."

Different leaders bring different skills, and as a result, different opportunities for innovation. An organization takes on the personality and giftedness of its leader. John and I are different in our personalities and our gift mix. He is what the Ranch needs in this season. He brings a unique perspective that I would not have brought during this time of my life.

In partnership with your Board of Directors, don't be afraid of thoughtful change. Embrace the need in your mission space and be willing to adjust accordingly.

SEASON TWO: LEADING

> ## KEY LESSON
>
> You should continually strive to innovate but, when possible, do so incrementally. Look for opportunities to elevate and transform your organization's services in strategic ways that will stand the test of time.
>
> *What are the core aspects of your historical mission to celebrate?*
> *What are some incremental steps to grow your organization?*

### INNOVATION AND INCREMENTALISM

I once asked a very successful businessman how he made decisions. He replied simply, "I make a lot of decisions really quickly and hope most of them will be right!"

I am a pragmatist and an incrementalist by nature. As much as possible, I like to segue into different innovations. For instance, before we started our on-campus school, we took four children who were underperforming in middle school and homeschooled them in our administration building.

The results were so positive—emotionally and educationally—we determined that to be good stewards of our children's lives, we needed to, at the very least, educate our middle school students on campus in modular units.

Five years later, we built a beautiful permanent school structure to educate children in grades 6-8. We then added 9th grade because it is so pivotal to a child's future academic success. A few years later, we brought all of our children on campus to provide schooling for elementary through high school. Most recently, we launched a day school program to serve students who need the academic support of our school but not full residential care. These incremental steps have allowed our program to grow to meet a proven need without getting ahead of our ability to execute well.

Launching a new initiative without a thorough vetting by staff and board members can be problematic, not just organizationally and culturally but also in the stewardship of financial resources.

I use this diagram to describe what an incremental approach to a new initiative might look like:

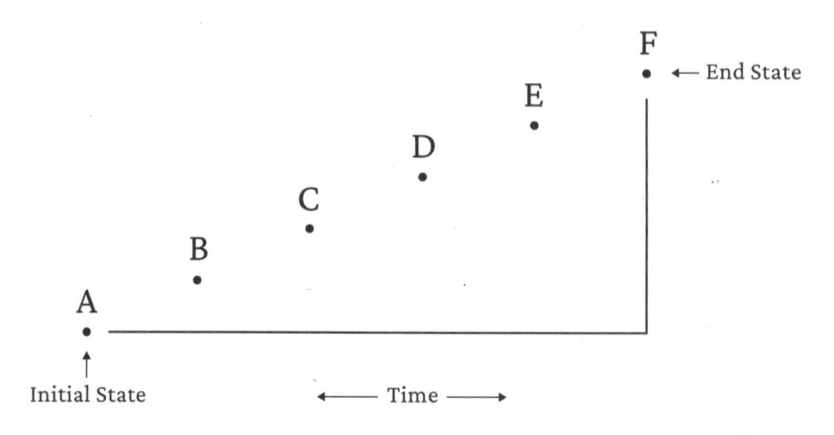

SEASON TWO: LEADING

A  Homeschooling for children
B  Purchased modular unit for grades 6-8
C  Construction of permanent on-campus school
D  Adding 9th grade to our on-campus school
E  Educating Eagle Ranch children in grades 2-12
F  Accepting non-residential children at Eagle Ranch School

**INNOVATION AND TRENDS**

With innovation, avoid gravitating toward trends that are not time-tested or aligned with your core mission. Industry trends can certainly enhance your mission. However, some trends originating from advocacy or governmental groups with limited practitioner experience can take you down some troublesome roads.

For example, I once worked with an individual who started a small but robust non-profit organization in the Southeast. During an initial visit, I was impressed by the difference he was making in his nonprofit space. Unfortunately, he shifted his programmatic focus, not once but twice, based on attractive trends that were financially lucrative. The funding for these new initiatives eventually dried up. As a result, his organization failed as well.

When considering industry trends, remember that you cannot be all things to all people. Many people will want to hitch their wagon to your successful organization. Saying "no" is one of the most powerful things a founder can do when these opportunities present themselves.

I have said "no" far more times than I have said "yes" to opportunities that on the surface seemed reasonable and attractive. In retrospect, pursuing them would have been an organizational distraction and greatly compromised our mission.

**INNOVATION AND DONORS**

Throughout our history, we have ascribed to the philosophy that "need drives vision." This belief promotes the best stewardship of the resources that God has entrusted to us. When we were considering The Wings Center as a new initiative, we also deliberated about two other worthy undertakings needed in our region. In the end, The Wings Center not only fulfilled the greatest need but also was the most congruent with our mission.

Unfortunately, a commitment to thoughtful and strategic growth can be short-circuited by a well-meaning donor or other third party.

This can manifest itself in a number of ways: donor pressure to pre-launch an initiative before the organization is operationally or culturally ready to assimilate that initiative into its mission; funding a project that isn't consistent with missional objectives; or undertaking an initiative that requires a disproportionate amount of organizational energy and focus. I have seen each of these scenarios compromise an organization's mission and effectiveness.

SEASON TWO: LEADING

> *I have said no far more times than I have said yes to opportunities that on the surface seemed reasonable and attractive.*

I have also witnessed highly respected organizations "go out of business" because they did not have the organizational or fiscal restraint to say no to what seemed like great opportunities but actually undermined their mission's core objectives.

Several years ago, I was contacted by a highly respected businessman and philanthropist. After observing the mission of Eagle Ranch for several years, he believed that the Ranch's therapeutic residential model could to be replicated throughout the country and even offered to fund the effort. We were certainly honored and humbled by this thoughtful offer, but we had already decided that our strategy for replicating our model was to help others start or retool existing child-caring programs, not to franchise.

Shortly thereafter, we had three different individuals/groups wanting to donate significant tracts of land in the Southeast for us to develop an "Eagle Ranch" in their area. Again, this was not consistent with our agreed-upon strategy, and we declined those offers as well.

To decline significant support is not an easy task. But overwhelmingly, most donors are *for* the mission, and many times they will be open to redirecting their funds toward a more pressing need.

SEASON TWO: LEADING

# Measuring Success

How do you measure success? I would venture to say the majority in the nonprofit arena define success anecdotally. It makes sense because people respond to stories. Many times, stories connect to our why, which resonates with people's hearts. Consequently, they give.

However, an increasing number of donors want quantifiable measures. This is primarily true in the foundation and corporate communities but is becoming increasingly prevalent with individual givers as well.

Not only is this trend important regarding fundraising, but it's also a stewardship issue. A question that needs to be asked and answered with integrity is this: "Are we effective in what we are doing with Kingdom resources, and if not, should we still exist or do we have the courage to change?"

### DEVELOPING MEASUREMENTS

It's easy to develop a positive perception with your constituency through your communications. Most people will never know whether or not an organization is a "paper tiger," that is, it looks great on the outside but does not have much substance in its operations. It really comes down to an integrity issue.

Developing quantifiable outcomes has been very much a process at Eagle Ranch with many recalibrations along the way.

We started off using a generic measurement tool but found it was difficult to interpret and didn't connect to our mission.

As a follow up, we designed a more tailored measurement system concentrating on several key indicators that unfortunately focused on a sample size that was too small.

Finally, we began to identify the key performance indicators for a child to be successful after their time at Eagle Ranch. For instance, two important indicators are a child's ability to self-regulate their emotions and an improvement in connecting relationally to family and others.

We designed the measurements to establish a baseline at entry into our program and then measured the child's progress every six months while they were with us. After leaving our program, we continue with more qualitative measurements at six and 18 months.

Some organizations do qualitative measurements two to five years after a child has left the program. Our argument for not testing that far out is that so many external factors could affect the child over that timeframe that you lose accuracy of the implications of their time in your program.

In the end, measures are as much for the organization as they are for your donors. Determine what constitutes success for the work you do, develop a tool to measure that success, and then decide how best to communicate

> *In the end,
> measures are as much
> for the organization
> as they are for
> your donors.*

those results to your supporters. Go a step further and share them with your staff to encourage them in their work, day-in and day-out.

> ## KEY LESSON
>
> Measuring your program's effectiveness is a stewardship issue. While success stories have impact, they need to be backed by quantitative measures. This can be achieved through industry measurements, client surveys, or measures developed around your program.
>
> *How do you define success for your mission?*
> *Can you measure it?*
> *How will you show you are successful?*

SEASON THREE

# Finishing

# *Finishing Thoughts*

THE book of Ecclesiastes says there is a season for everything and a time for every activity (3:1). There is a time for founding, a time for leading, and a time for finishing. We are called to be good stewards of each season.

In 2015, I began thinking more about my succession plan and coming to grips with the eventual finality of my time as executive director. So, at age 60, I pulled aside our chairman of the board, and said, "I think in five years, we need to have named my replacement." It seemed like an innocuous comment at the time, but it set in motion a process for which I was not emotionally prepared. A part of me wanted to go back to the board and say, "Maybe I could stay just a little longer." But I had a strong feeling that this was God's timing for me. Secondly, I sensed almost immediately the board's increased ownership of the Ranch mission. They were ready to engage deeply in this process, both through prayer and planning.

The finishing season can be challenging, especially to a founder. The faith to let go and trust God with what is next makes the finishing process inherently difficult. Maybe that is why founder transitions are so often ignored or poorly executed in both the for-profit and nonprofit worlds.

In this season, I think one of two perspectives can emerge and will determine the difference between a problematic or a healthy transition. Do you, as a founder, see this season as an opportunity to position your organization through a new leader, to grow beyond your own giftedness and capabilities? Or, is your identity and self-worth so tied to the mission that truly letting go is not an option, thereby crippling the opportunity for organizational growth?

Finishing well is a journey. I hope the following pages will encourage you along the way.

# Planning for Succession

## Founding with the Finish in Mind

Whether you're reading this book before starting a nonprofit organization or well into the journey, a founder should always have the end in sight.

There are practical reasons for this foresight. No organization should be solely dependent on the health and well-being of its leader. We tend to laugh when others ask, "What would happen to your organization if you got hit by a bus tomorrow?" But in all seriousness, do you have an answer to this question?

Too often, succession is barely an afterthought for many founders. Beyond purchasing keyman life insurance and signing off on basic organizational adjustments should the unexpected occur, many organizations avoid, delay, or ignore the difficult thinking and conversations around successful succession planning. While the following insights focus on a strategically-planned succession when the founder gives notice of retiring, many considerations remain the same for an unplanned or emergency succession.

### GETTING A HEAD START

The average tenure of a founder is 32 years, and 63.5 is the average age at retirement/transition. I can attest to the fact that actively positioning your organization—and yourself—for succession is some of the hardest work you'll ever do. Because of this, founders delay this process and typically stay two to three years past their effectiveness (or one or more bad decisions longer than they should). I didn't want that to be my story.

I've seen several of my peers hang on too long, finally letting go in a weakened state. There is a significant difference between "letting go" (exhausted) and "handing off" (strategic).

To position an organization for a leadership transition, I encourage founders to begin considering the organizational implications of succession 10 years prior to retirement or moving on to what's next in their lives. This provides adequate time to address myriad succession issues and questions, and to pass on a strong, healthy organization.

*There is a significant difference between letting go (exhausted) and handing off (strategic).*

While the initial conversation and planning stage started earlier at Eagle Ranch, specifics about hiring and putting the succession wheels in motion began five years before my planned departure. That's when I let our board of directors know I was ready to start the more formal process. This advance notice allowed a realistic and adequate timeline to hire the right person and make a smooth transition.

I don't want to give the impression that I handed off a neat and tidy package to my successor. Loose ends are inevitable, and I had to be okay with that scenario. I could have stayed on several more years, but I realized that extra time wouldn't have made an appreciable difference or benefited the succession process.

The great thing about leaving "early" is that you have the energy to be an ambassador or advisor for your successor. I also was able to move confidently into a new career chapter that continues to give me purpose and excitement about the future. Had I stayed until I was burned out, none of this would have been possible.

God told Abraham to go. He didn't give him a lot of time but just wanted him to move on to the next season (Genesis 12:1).

> **KEY LESSON**
>
> It's never too soon to start thinking about succession. A succession plan should be an ongoing board/executive director discussion in case of an unplanned event. For planned succession from a founder to the next executive director, transition plans should start well before the founder is ready to move on.
>
> *How will you define personal success when you are no longer at the helm?*
> *How will you define organizational success when you are no longer at the helm?*
> *What are your plans for a smooth, strategic "handoff" rather than an "exhausted" letting go?*

## Planning for the Transition

Choosing an ideal "retirement" date allows you (and the organization) sufficient time for planning. If you stay on too long, organizational continuity is disrupted.

I had a friend in the nonprofit space who stayed on as executive director until he was almost 80 years old. Consequently, at least two generations of leadership were not leveraged at this organization. Needless to say, when he was replaced, they were significantly behind in technology advancements and industry trends that happened during his tenure. The organization never recovered.

My advice would be to consider leaving a year before you think you are truly ready. This enables you to go out strong and have energy for the transition. I looked at my transition not as an addendum to my career, but rather the most important aspect of it.

### A STRONG BASELINE

Putting a stake in the ground regarding leadership transition enables you to work backward to create expectations around organizational goals, staffing, and fundraising. This timeline allows room to begin "clearing the decks" of any major issues to ensure that you are leaving the organization in as sound a position as possible—organizationally, culturally and financially—for the successor to step into. However, few nonprofit organizations ever truly achieve a sound footing. There is always something amiss, whether it be an aging donor base, a culture/strategy gap, a weak board or other challenges. Many of these issues are long-term in nature, so consider several principles.

First, don't let long-term challenges become an excuse for an overly long delay in leadership transition. Second, develop the criteria/attributes for candidates that give

SEASON THREE: FINISHING

> *I looked at my transition not as an addendum to my career, but rather the most important aspect of it.*

you confidence in their ability to address these long-term challenges.

In my experience the following needs to be in place before a transition:

- Stable funding base
- Exceptional and committed senior level staff
- A board of directors committed to ownership of the mission and the transition process
- Lean organizational structure/staffing

While you are evaluating the current state of the organization, address succession issues with all senior level staff. What is *their* projected career timeline as the current executive director's tenure comes to an end?

### ORGANIZATIONAL IMPACT

Setting up your organization for a successful transition may necessitate a potential change within the organization's structure and staff roles. Due to the inevitable differences in leadership style from a founder to successor, the outgoing executive director has a responsibility to keep the organization as lean as possible. A lean organization allows the successor to step in and staff the organization to fit his or her own giftedness and management style.

I once consulted with a nonprofit whose retiring executive director left a bloated organization, which meant his successor had to terminate 50 percent of the staff due to inefficiency and financial pressures. As a result, this incoming executive director had to deal with the fallout from these terminations before launching a new organizational vision.

During the few years prior to succession, your job as the founder is twofold. First, make sure that anyone who is not aligned with the mission is moved on. The successor doesn't need to inherit people who are problematic regarding the vision of the organization. Second, if possible, do not add new staff in the last year leading up to the transition so the new leader can make his or her own hires.

### KEY LESSON

Choose a retirement date so that you can work backward to position your organization for success during a transition in leadership.

*How do you feel about a future leadership transition? Begin the process by discussing this with a trusted confidant.
How might succession impact the organizational structure?*

## The Role of the Board

Eagle Ranch is a board-led organization. As discussed in an earlier chapter, successful organizations with longevity empower a board to make key decisions and ultimately have authority over a founder/executive director.

Our board owned the important responsibilities of the succession process—planning, hiring, and helping the new leader get established to make his own mark on the organization within set boundaries.

Board members are owners and gatekeepers of the mission. The board has a strategic responsibility to leverage its collective IQ to make an intelligent hire that ensures the health and future of the organization. The board should own the succession strategy and work as a team with the outgoing executive director to execute. Pat MacMillan's book *Mission Centered Governance* reinforces this key point:

*"Selecting a chief executive officer for any organization, particularly one that is pursuing the purposes of God, may be the most important task of any ministry board."*

In preparation for a transition, the board should have an understanding in a multitude of areas to ensure the organization is in a sound position for the planning process. Board discussion should follow these guidelines:

SEASON THREE: FINISHING

- What is the defined role of the board in the succession process?

- What is currently going on within the organization (challenges/opportunities)?

- Are vision possibilities for the next 10-15 years outlined? What are the attributes, values, qualities and skills needed by a leader to move the organization toward the vision?

- How will succession impact the organizational structure? Do any adjustments need to be made?

- Is there an internal staff member qualified and willing to step into the position?

- If an external hire is necessary, how will this be approached and managed?

- How will you communicate the transition to your staff, clients, donors, and other key audiences?

- What is the leadership transition timeframe? Is it more immediate or sequenced?

## PLANNED VS. UNPLANNED SUCCESSION

The board of directors should view succession not as a singular event but as an ongoing process. It needs to be addressed at regular intervals, especially as it pertains to planned versus unplanned succession scenarios. The book *Mission Centered Governance* further states:

> *"Hopefully an unplanned or forced transition (e.g., an accident or an unexpected resignation or termination) won't happen, but wise boards have a plan in place if it does. Such a plan (e.g., needed attributes in a leader, possible internal and external candidates) is reviewed annually in the board's executive sessions. For planned transitions, it is hoped that a strong internal candidate might be available. However, such situations seldom just happen. They are a product of planning and long-term preparation as possible candidates are identified and developed over time in collaboration with the chief executive. This transition strategy too becomes a topic for regular review by the board."*

In addition to this succession planning, defining the ongoing "partnership" between the board of directors and a new organizational leader is of paramount importance. The roles and responsibilities of the board and the new leader should be defined clearly but are often not addressed.

SEASON THREE: FINISHING

## KEY LESSON

Your board of directors has a responsibility to partner with you in a leadership transition to carry the organization into the future.

*Have you defined the role of your board in
the succession process?
Do you have plans in place for both planned and
unplanned succession scenarios?*

TAKE A DEEPER LOOK AT THE PARTNERSHIP BETWEEN A NEW ORGANIZATIONAL LEADER AND THE BOARD.

# The Search

## Defining the Ideal Successor

### VISION FOR THE FUTURE

As you pull together job criteria and ideal attributes for a potential successor, you must first define a clearer picture of the "now" and potential future scenarios for your organization. Will aspects of your mission change? How could your program expand? What societal factors may impact the clientele you serve?

Just as the organization began with an initial vision, that vision will continue to evolve over time as the baton passes to the next generation of leadership. Having an idea of varying vision possibilities for the organization will assist you in mapping out the ideal qualities and traits of a future successor.

### AGE MAKES A DIFFERENCE

There are differences between someone undertaking a mission in their younger years and those more seasoned. Of course, the obvious ones with younger leaders are more energy, creativity, and technological skills, just to name a few. However, limited life experience can be challenging, so it is of particular importance they surround themselves with truth tellers to keep them inside the missional guardrails. Though painful at the time, my board of directors kept me from going down some troublesome roads that I was convinced were the right way to go. I just didn't know what I didn't know.

With older leaders, their previous successes aren't necessarily transferable to a new venture. Their maturity and life experience can certainly be a positive in the development of a nonprofit organization; however, because of presumed limited tenure (due to age), creating and establishing sustainable systems and processes can be problematic. They can also be challenged with emerging technology trends.

Where an organization is in its life cycle can give a valuable perspective on how to proceed with this decision.

## DEVELOPING JOB CRITERIA

The executive director and search committee should create weighted criteria and a job description for the position. It's critical to define the job description in one to two pages, keeping qualifications clear and concise regarding the specific skills and competencies needed.

A few things to keep in mind as you are drafting your criteria and job description:

- Distinguish between the "must-haves" and the "like-to-haves."

- Avoid usage of internal "corporate speak" that an external candidate will not understand.

- Don't overestimate portability of skills from one job to the next as an indicator of future performance. Emotional awareness/intelligence (EQ) may be among the biggest drivers of senior leadership success.

- Seek someone who embraces the historical ethos, enjoys maintaining and developing internal systems, and desires to innovate.

- Look for giftedness and experience in management of the scale for which they are being hired.

### SAME BUT DIFFERENT

The successor will most likely have a different mindset, style and skillset than the founder. However, it's critically important to identify the core parts of the organization's DNA that need to be replicated in the new leader. Certain commonalities must exist to respect and keep the culture moving forward in a positive way.

First, the new leader must have a *passion* for the mission, values and priorities of the organization. Seek to discern the difference between an individual's passion for the mission versus a mere understanding and acquiescence to the mission.

Second, it is paramount to find someone who is a cultural fit. This is where new hires "rise or fall."

Third, soft skills and character traits often take a backseat to education and experience but are just as, if not more, important. A few examples include servant leadership, humility, open-mindedness, insight, determination, curiosity and potential.

Finally, "contextual" experience, especially as it pertains to leading a faith-based venture, is a foundational consideration. Do they have experience in seeing God's provision, and have they personally experienced the power of the Holy Spirit in helping them carry out a calling?

SEASON THREE: FINISHING

> *Identify the core parts of the organization's DNA that need to be replicated in the new leader.*

> **KEY LESSON**
>
> Ensure that you have a broad vision for the organization's future before you determine the traits and qualities needed in the successor. Take your time developing a thorough job description. The successor may look different from the founder, but core aspects of his or her DNA should be the same.
>
> *Have you identified the core aspects of the organization's DNA that need to be present in your successor?*
> *Are vision possibilities for the next 10-15 years outlined?*
> *What are the attributes of a leader who can move the vision forward?*

## The Selection Process

### THE SEARCH

On average, the search for a new executive director takes 12-18 months. Search firms can be effective but may eventually be just part of the search process.

SEASON THREE: FINISHING

The best strategy is to develop criteria that you "carry around" as an ongoing vetting process for those with whom you interact. It gives valuable definition to what you are looking for and a ready explanation of the characteristics of the ideal candidate. During this process, I literally looked at these criteria once a week, thinking about who might be a candidate.

While the executive director may be involved in the search process, they should not drive it. As explained earlier, this process needs to be owned by the board of directors since they will be living and working with whomever the successor will be.

### INTERNAL VS EXTERNAL HIRES

There are pros and cons in an internal vs. external hire for such a crucial role in your organization. As a general rule, internal successors have higher success rates than external candidates because of their cultural alignment, organizational knowledge, and less onboarding (integration) time. Additionally, you can have a more accurate view of how they match up against the established criteria. Unfortunately, your evaluation of an internal candidate might be skewed because of their current role in the organization being materially different from the role of executive director.

You should always benchmark an internal candidate against external candidates to ensure that you select the most qualified person.

When hiring externally, cultural fit is one of the most important criteria. Education, job titles, and past experiences can be overweighted, while the intangibles or soft skills—social integration and the ability to amass social equity in order to lead effectively—are some of the more important qualities. A big upside of an external hire is fresh ideas, especially when an organization is struggling.

With an external hire, crossover with the previous executive director will be longer. You should also consider a strategic orientation and gradual assimilation process, which will substantially increase their "stick" rate.

**THE INTERVIEW PROCESS**

As you begin to narrow your focus on specific candidates, the interview process begins. This process should be well-thought-out and planned with specific, targeted questions that will cover all the desired characteristics in your ideal candidate.

At this point, you should have identified a key selection committee to lead the charge in selecting the replacement. This selection committee should include current and past board members with cognitive diversity (different ways of assessing and processing). Choose individuals who are experienced at interviewing and adept at asking tough, probing, and behavioral/experience-based questions.

During these interviews, define an individual's career

trajectory based on experience, performance and potential. Most organizations do a good job with the first two but, unfortunately, a poor job of evaluating potential. You should not only look at the current state of someone's career, but at their potential to grow both professionally and personally. As mentioned earlier regarding vision, your organizational environment will not remain the same. If the person is assessed for potential, it usually coincides with discovering a person's deepest motive rather than a "real-time" role that may or may not be a good fit for your mission.

As you move further into the interview process, make sure to prioritize background checks. Conduct your due diligence in getting additional outside perspectives on the candidate, both professionally and personally. Psychological assessment tools (like DiSC, Myers-Briggs, The Predictive Index) administered by a professional also provide valuable insight.

There are four ways to acquire information about a candidate: interview, references, resume and psychological testing. For a CEO-level position, you should generally use all four when making a selection because the risks of getting it wrong are so high.

A rushed or poorly-executed process for this crucial role can have long lasting negative implications for an organization that may take many years to remedy.

> ### KEY LESSON
>
> Take your time in the search process. Consider benchmarking internal and external candidates to make the best selection for your organization.
>
> *Is there an internal staff member qualified and willing to step into the position?*
> *If an external hire is a necessary consideration, how will this be approached and managed?*

## How We Found My Successor

After 12 months of recruiting efforts, our search firm had been unable to find my successor. It certainly wasn't because of a lack of effort. A number of competent individuals surfaced, but we felt none of them had strong alignment with our why or with our culture.

That first year of our search was laborious. Some people even commented that based on our candidate criteria, we were looking for a "needle in a haystack." But we were committed to finding that "needle" regardless of how long it took.

I believe each of us is a reflection of the people with whom we associate. Similarly, if we are seeking an indi-

## SEASON THREE: FINISHING

vidual who embodies the core parts of our organizational DNA, the best place to begin looking is those closest to us.

This philosophy ultimately led to identifying John Shackelford as my successor. The story of how we found John unfolded something like this.

One day, I was on the phone with my good friend, David Salyers, who asked how the search was going. David is a 37-year marketing veteran with Chick-fil-A. As Eagle Ranch's first board member he was instrumental in helping me in our early days.

As we spoke, David asked what type of person we were looking for to fill the Executive Director role. Here is how he tells the story:

*"I guess the Lord prompted me—I just thought of John Shackelford. And the more Eddie described what he was looking for, the more excited I got because in so many ways John is a lot like Eddie. Eddie was always mature and wise beyond his years. For a younger man, John has an old soul. I've always thought about John as a great leader, and he's always had a heart to serve. He and Eddie are cut from the same cloth.*

*The primary characteristic John shares with Eddie is humility. Eddie is smart, charismatic, wise and has so much to offer, but all of that is balanced with his humility. I think the same thing about John. He seeks first to listen. He encourages others. People want to follow John.*

*There is a strong desire to serve God that I've seen in Eddie's life, and I've seen in John's life. They are both motivated by mission."*

It seems fitting that the Ranch's first board member would identify our next executive director. I think David saw in John a combination of skill and heart that uniquely qualified him for the role.

When I met John, I immediately liked him and could see why David identified him as a candidate. It might seem like John's qualifications and the recommendation of a highly respected friend would make him a shoo-in. But we put John through the same rigorous process that every prior candidate had experienced. This not only helped ensure John was the right fit for us but that we were the right fit for him—and that Eagle Ranch was the place he actually wanted to be.

After four months filled with interviews, meetings with senior staff, psychological testing, and reference checks, we were ready to offer John the position. He had a lot to consider: resigning from a high-level position with one of the nation's top companies; leaving a community and friends he cared about in the heart of Atlanta; and perhaps hardest of all, moving his growing family to an unfamiliar area and, in a sense, starting over.

I was impressed with what ultimately helped John make his decision to join Eagle Ranch: obedience to God's

SEASON THREE: FINISHING

calling on his life. (In a later chapter, John shares his recollections about being asked to apply for the executive director position and his call to serve.)

As I've noted throughout this book, the passing of the baton to John has been both rewarding and challenging (for both of us!). Without question, John embodies the fundamental ethos and organizational DNA of Eagle Ranch.

> ### KEY LESSON
>
> When recruiting candidates for a successor or other key positions, seek input and support from the people closest to you.
>
> *Who knows you and your organization well enough to help identify the "right fit" for your successor?*

# Making a Successful Transition

### Getting Started

Hiring the right person is not the finish line. It's the starting line. First and foremost, your successor needs to be someone you genuinely like and respect. Otherwise, there will be a tendency to avoid and not engage your successor in their learning curve, and becoming their ambassador will be difficult. Most importantly, your staff will also be able to sense that you are not fully on board with your successor.

Secondly, as mentioned earlier, the new leader must be in cultural alignment with the mission. This easily

*Hiring the right person is not the finish line. It's the starting line.*

SEASON THREE: FINISHING

trumps educational background and experience. If someone is not aligned culturally, all types of issues will arise to make their ability to lead difficult, if not impossible. A leader who is misaligned culturally will usually experience a mass exodus of the existing staff.

Another important consideration is that the successor respects the history of the mission they are inheriting. But a high-quality leader must also be positioned to do more than just maintain the mission—there needs to be an eye toward innovation to keep the ministry relevant. Innovation needs to be a "respecter of history," thoughtful, and under the guidance of the board of directors.

The successor should understand that the mission is owned by the board of directors and be willing to defer to the board's leadership. The board's role is to protect the new leader and the mission from ill-advised decisions and to encourage and support purposeful and collaborative innovation.

**COMMUNICATING THE CHANGE**

Once the selection is made, a carefully planned announcement should be prepared to inform your staff, donors, constituents, volunteers, and other key stakeholders.

Internally, a formal business meeting should be held with staff to announce the transition but also to ease fears about what such a change could cause. This announcement should cover why the transition is happening, who was selected and why, and what the onboarding plan will look like. The outgoing executive director should handle this communication with the staff. It provides a tangible sign-off in support of the new leader: "This is my person to lead our mission forward." Individual conversations can be held "offline" to provide additional reassurance to concerned staff members.

Externally, a rollout package should be developed to include a formal press release, website updates, images and content for social media, email content, and an informative piece of collateral to mail out to key constituents. There should also be strategic interactions with select local media outlets. To take things a step further, you could also consider the development of a video. (This could be just a profile on the successor or a Q&A dialogue between the founder and successor.) Communicating directly with your audiences will prevent information from being misrepresented or misconstrued.

SEASON THREE: FINISHING

## KEY LESSON

Remember that hiring the right person is not the finish line but the starting line. Trust that you have done your due diligence throughout the selection process to help arrive at a decision. Communicate with all audiences about how, when, and why the transition in leadership is occurring.

*Do you believe in the selection process
you have developed?
What is your strategy to communicate the
transition in leadership to your staff,
donors, clients and other key audiences?*

VIEW EAGLE RANCH'S LEADERSHIP TRANSITION BROCHURE.

## Onboarding and Assimilation

Races are won or lost with the baton pass. You don't want to hold on too long or let go too quickly.

The transition of leadership at Eagle Ranch in 2021 was unique. Although we made an external hire, many of the cultural qualities we hoped for were manifested in our hire of John Shackelford, who had been employed at Chick-fil-A for 10 years. Although every transition scenario will be different, onboarding and assimilation of an external hire will need to be much more in-depth than for an internal hire (who would already have institutional knowledge and cultural integration).

I would recommend a gradual handoff from the current executive director to his or her successor based on previous experience and skills. For instance, if the successor has a background in public relations or finance, those processes would be handed off in the near term as opposed to perhaps program services and physical plant operations. Most likely, the last area to be handed off would be in the fundraising realm as the current executive director's many relationships will need to be transferred strategically and over time to the new executive director.

The successor needs to learn the different aspects of the mission from the ground up, especially the processes that are missional in nature. For instance, understanding, appreciating, and interacting with those on the frontlines builds tremendous organizational equity, not just with the frontline workers but with everyone else who is observing the onboarding process. Existing staff members are watching to see if the successor is willing to get into the missional trenches.

Start with a basic onboarding plan and collapse or expand it according to the person's competencies and learning curve.

Crossover with the outgoing organizational leader gives the staff confidence in the successor. In contrast to the conventional wisdom of a one- to three-month transitional overlap, a 12- to 18-month overlap can be more appropriate with a complex organization with an especially sensitive culture. A longer onboarding timeframe allows for more significant assimilation. This can also be a litmus test of humility for the new leader.

## FIRST ORDER OF BUSINESS

First, the new executive director needs to be in a posture of listening and learning. The integration of all the processes that drive a nonprofit can be complex. Observing this complexity in the early days of their tenure will help immensely in mitigating poor decision-making.

Second, the successor should establish an internal meeting schedule with the senior leadership team and staff. This could be a mix of individual and group meetings. Ideally, these meetings happen within the first month of their new role. From then on, the successor should interact with all direct reports and their reports on a regular basis. During these initial meetings, you need to assess the dynamic between the founder and successor to determine how successful joint communications and meetings will be.

Third, the successor should meet individually with every board member and advisory board member. After all, these are the owners of the mission, and they need to know the new executive director not just through the interview process but personally. Identify a board "advocate" who will assist with the transition process and provide ongoing support.

Finally, create a positive "enduring impression" with your external audience that is carried forward in the midst of a transition. Consider joint speaking engagements with the founder introducing the successor to local churches, civic clubs, and other organizations.

The founder should also introduce the successor to key donors and constituents. This could be a great cultivation opportunity as these stakeholders will be the first to get to know your replacement.

TAKE A CLOSER LOOK AT THE LEADERSHIP TRANSITION AT EAGLE RANCH FROM EDDIE STAUB TO JOHN SHACKELFORD.

SEASON THREE: FINISHING

> ### KEY LESSON
>
> Races are won or lost with the baton pass. There is danger in holding on too long or letting go too quickly. Start with a basic onboarding and assimilation plan. Collapse or expand it according to the successor's competencies and learning curve.
>
> *Have you created an onboarding and assimilation timeline?*
> *What are the first orders of business for the successor in your organization?*

## Become an Ambassador

It is natural for your staff, board, and key stakeholders to have some hesitation and fear about a new executive director, especially one taking the place of a founder.

One of the best ways to set up your successor for a positive transition is to be their ambassador, showing your confidence in them to lead the organization into a new era. For a founder with a lot of equity inside and outside the organization, signing off on the successor's agenda can be very powerful.

## AVOIDING THE "SHADOW OF THE FOUNDER"

As the successor settles into their new role, the former executive director should deliberately diminish his or her own influence and increase the visibility and influence of the successor.

It will be natural (and expected) for others in the organization to look to the former executive director for direction and approval, but the danger is that it disempowers the successor. From a business perspective, there *must* be a separation of roles, especially if the founder is staying on with the organization in a different capacity. The two must work in tandem to agree on boundaries as well as a timetable. Some questions to address include:

- What does the runway for the founder look like regarding engagement to disengagement?

- Does the founder continue to attend board meetings?

- Do your staff directors immediately report to the successor, or is there a crossover period?

Being an ambassador for the successor also means being confident enough in their leadership to step aside, even when you might not agree with a decision.

SEASON THREE: FINISHING

*One of the best ways to set up your successor for a positive transition is to be their ambassador.*

## A SUCCESSFUL FOUNDER/SUCCESSOR RELATIONSHIP

A transition of this magnitude necessitates a positive working relationship. In part, this is facilitated by regular meetings between the outgoing executive director and successor. Make this a priority. Sometimes those meetings are a continuance of building a personal relationship, and it provides an opportunity for the successor to leverage the long-term experience of an outgoing executive director. It can also diffuse misunderstandings should one get into the other person's "stuff."

---

### KEY LESSON

Being an ambassador for the new leader is critical for their effectiveness with staff, board members, donors, and the community. A positive relationship with the outgoing executive director will go a long way to empowering the successor as they step into their new role.

*How can you ensure a successful working relationship with your successor?*

SEASON THREE: FINISHING

# Passing the Baton

### THE REALITIES AND DIFFICULTIES OF LEAVING

Letting go of something you started and worked hard at for so many years does not come without difficulty. No one can fully appreciate how founders have felt the weight of the organization from day one. Founders themselves may not even realize this ongoing pressure until relieved of their current role.

After nearly 40 years as the executive director of Eagle Ranch, I understand the struggle that comes with letting go—especially as the founder of an organization. Post-succession can be an unsettling time as leaders grapple with their identity and affirmation apart from leading an organization they started.

You know in your head that it's time to step aside, but it takes a while for your heart to catch up. Handle this with as much integrity and accountability as possible. It is advisable to preach to yourself *daily*, especially if you've experienced a long tenure with an organization.

Remember the God who called you to start an organization is also the one who releases you. Stay attuned to the Holy Spirit regarding timing and expectant of what the next season might look like.

*The God who called you to start an organization is also the one who releases you.*

SEASON THREE: FINISHING

### SOME WORDS OF WISDOM

These thoughts were garnered over the years from friends and mentors who have passed the baton:

- Consider 10 goals you want to accomplish before stepping down, but be okay if not all are completed. Everything doesn't need to be neat and tidy at handoff. There will always be loose ends.

- To accelerate integration for the successor, prepare an analysis of the organization. I listed over 25 challenges and opportunities.

- Provide a thorough understanding and background of the key stakeholders for your successor. Making personal introductions to key donors and stakeholders is important.

- "Clear the decks" of any major issues so the successor doesn't step into a tough situation.

- Don't take on new "big" projects in the one to two years before you plan to leave.

- The new leader moves into the executive director office and is the organizational leader on day one. If you are staying on in a peripheral capacity, you need an office in a completely different building, if possible, to create some separation. If you live on campus, consider moving. There is a lot to be said about physically relocating before you formally transition roles.

- Consider taking some time off after the transition to regroup emotionally and begin to reflect on what God has next for you. He is not through with you yet. You're just entering a new season.

- Nothing is wrong with a gradual letting go, but you don't need to second-guess your replacement. They will have different gifts and perceptions than you, and you need to be okay with that.

- Finally, let the new leader make mistakes. That's how they will best learn.

SEASON ONE: FOUNDING

> ## KEY LESSON
>
> Moving on is difficult. Remember, God is in the process of writing our story. You are not going to be less purposeful going forward. Leverage your years of experience for broader influence.
>
> *Where could your next season be taking you?*

John Shackelford, Executive Director of Eagle Ranch
and Eddie Staub, Founder. 2024

# Closing Perspectives

## Transition— A Founder's Perspective

BY EDDIE STAUB

As I considered my future succession, I was struck by how few organizations in both the nonprofit and for-profit space do leadership transition well. I decided to become a student of transitions. I wanted finishing well to be one of the most important aspects of my tenure as executive director and not just an addendum.

I believe that a successful transition starts with simply liking and respecting your successor. As mentioned in an earlier chapter, competency is just part of the equation. I would argue that cultural fit is far more important. In our search process we interviewed many competent individuals who were not a good cultural fit. Because we had no internal candidate, we knew we would have to go external in our search, recognizing that external hires are statistically a 50/50 proposition. Fortunately, my successor, John Shackelford, was from Chick-fil-A, an organization that shares many of our cultural values. As a result, John felt almost like an internal hire for us.

There is also the dynamic of the founder/successor relationship and ongoing interaction. Understandably, a candidate might have a concern about me, the founder, still being around for a season, even if it was in a parallel venture. When John was asked about that founder scenario, he responded, "I'm not sure I would be interested in this job if the founder wasn't still around." That spoke to a number of traits that we valued in John: humility, teachability, and a security in his own giftedness.

John and I also laid out an agreed-upon transition timetable but realized that it could ebb and flow based on his learning curve and assimilation at the Ranch. For instance, we shortened the timeline in several areas, while others were extended by six months to a year.

In the midst of these boundaries, we were committed to honest conversations, thinking the best of each other. In the course of our transition, we have both gotten into each other's stuff (me more than John), have readily apologized and moved on. As the founder, I was used to operating a train going 90 miles per hour. It's difficult just to exit and not be carried ahead by momentum into areas that once were under my purview. John has been very gracious and understanding.

I knew when John was hired that he would want to innovate. It was important to me that any innovation respected the rich history of Eagle Ranch. John has been masterful in balancing this. We need to change. We've continually evolved over our decades-long history, going from a boys' ranch to also serving girls, to an on-campus school, equine therapy, and now The Wings Center, which provides community counseling along with retreats and Wings Consulting. Eagle Ranch would be much less than it is today if we weren't open to innovation. Moving forward, there will be opportunities for us to get better at what we do and plow new ground for God's Kingdom.

Prior to John's hiring, the board of directors developed some organizational guidelines and parameters. This keeps the board from micro-managing and allows the Ranch to remain open and receptive to new ideas.

My relationship with the board over our history has been almost symbiotic, working hand-in-glove to develop the Ranch mission. In moving from the "boss" of a long-term founder to overseeing a new executive director, it's critical that the board be even more aware of its strategic responsibilities and fiscal oversight as they come alongside John in developing the future direction of Eagle Ranch.

Another thing that John has done so well is to gravitate toward the mission itself. It would be much easier to start his new role focused on business operations and external opportunities that are not as intense and the learning curve not as steep. Intuitively, John knew that the rubber meets the road with our children and families. Consequently, he has pursued learning in that area with tenacity and humility.

It benefits any successor to start in the trenches to understand the heart of the mission. This galvanizes their leadership equity with staff, which is crucial in mission execution.

In closing, my greatest desire in this transition was to be an ambassador for John, both internally and externally, and be his biggest cheerleader. However, I never thought about how important it would be for John to also be an ambassador for me as I moved forward into my next season. He has done that with grace and intentionality.

## Transition— A Successor's Perspective

BY JOHN SHACKELFORD
EAGLE RANCH EXECUTIVE DIRECTOR, 2021-

Eddie Staub's legacy is incredible, and one of his most powerful and lasting legacies will be how he is finishing at Eagle Ranch.

## SEASON THREE: FINISHING

When I left my corporate career and my family left our home in the city to participate in God's calling for us at Eagle Ranch, many thought we had lost our minds. In fairness to them, many founder transitions do not go well, and some of our friends loved us too much to see us walk into what they expected would be a very unhealthy situation. Admittedly, I had my fears but felt much more comfortable after an illuminating and transparent four-month interview process.

As I write this, I am just over a year into leading Eagle Ranch as its second-ever executive director. Eddie and I have enjoyed a beautiful friendship and partnership that I think has made each of us better while greatly benefiting the mission and impact of Eagle Ranch. There are many things that could and should be said about this process. But I feel the most important contribution I can make to this discussion is to clarify that while it "takes two to tango" in a transition, I believe it's a lot more about how the founder handles the transition than the successor.

The successor can be a model citizen in every way, but if the founder doesn't proactively support the new leader, preparing him or her for the transition, then disaster is imminent. Thankfully for me and Eagle Ranch, Eddie has been an intentional and humble servant-leader. Specifically, I'd like to note three ways in which Eddie is finishing well in this transition season.

First, Eddie and the Eagle Ranch board were deliberate, intentional, and prayerful about the transition. Eddie began praying about his successor 10 years before I entered the process. That means he was praying for me as I was starting my career at Chick-fil-A in 2011...amazing! All decisions should be bathed in prayer, but when it comes to succession planning, it's easy for gifted leaders to take matters into their own hands. I was consistently impressed by how much the Holy Spirit, not a controlling board member or founder, seemed to be leading this process.

Secondly, Eddie and the board had a clear and well-articulated plan for what he would do in the transition. Rather than a "wait and see" approach, they had clearly outlined for Eddie to help launch Eagle Ranch's new initiative, The Wings Center. This gave him a clear reason to still be involved at the Ranch while having a specific new job that energized him—and it gave me the space needed to fully lead in my new role.

Lastly, Eddie took specific actions to symbolize (both to himself and the broader community) that it was time for him to step into a new season. In Eddie's case, this happened primarily through two key moves:

1. Eddie and his wife moved off the Ranch (where they had lived their entire married lives) to allow me and my family to move in.

SEASON THREE: FINISHING

2. Eddie moved his office from our administrative building to The Wings Center on our campus, allowing me to occupy the executive director office and the space to lead my new team.

Both moves were powerful symbols of change and acts of humility. Eddie's courage to humble himself in these ways has paid incredible dividends in allowing our culture to move forward.

Each leadership transition is unique. The specifics of how it should be handled depend on many factors, but I strongly believe the principles that Eddie has shared in this book (and that he has lived out) are transferrable. Ultimately, I believe it comes down to humility.

As a leader, are you willing to acknowledge that all of your power, influence, and authority comes from a sovereign, loving God? Do you believe the mission is much bigger than you, and are you willing to lead in a way that doesn't make the organization dependent on you? My life and the generational impact on children and families in crisis are so much richer as a result of Eddie Staub's humility and courage to trust Jesus with his life's work. Praise be to the Lord!

## What's Next— Continued Purpose

For the founder, "what's next" can be very challenging. What was important to me—beyond a commitment to a smooth transition for my successor—was to believe that God was not through with me in regard to bearing fruit for the Kingdom. The next season for a founder can be as fruitful as the previous season of leading an organization. It will just look different.

God always wants to birth something new in us, and we need to be spiritually expectant as to what a new season may look like.

I believe God's plan is to take us from "strength to strength" (Psalm 84:7). Many times, previous experiences and knowledge provide a touchpoint, a launching pad into our next endeavor. For me, it was to establish Wings Consulting, where I consult with other children's programs and nonprofits based on my learning and experiences at Eagle Ranch.

Moving into a new season requires a "letting go" of the old season. This can be especially difficult when your successor does things in a different way (not wrong, just different). Someone once said, "Nothing grows in the founder's shadow." I believe that can be true, especially if the founder is hovering over their successor. Conversely, the founder can also be helpful in coming alongside to give ad-

## SEASON THREE: FINISHING

vice. Based on past experiences, the founder sees the hazards and road bumps along the way that can help their successor forego a lot of pain. However, some lessons are best learned the hard way, and the founder needs to be secure enough to let things unfold without intervening.

What has helped me throughout this process is that I had a parallel venture with defined boundaries and responsibilities at Eagle Ranch. Consequently, John and I meet at least every two weeks to discuss issues that need to be processed. I also attend Eagle Ranch executive committee meetings and board meetings. Otherwise, I am occupied with consulting and oversight of The Wings Center. My successor knows I am always available in the interim.

I think it would be much more difficult if there were not a substantive role for the founder but rather an ill-defined, speaking role for the organization. In those cases, the value of the founder being around is limited and should be short-lived. It can be difficult watching someone else leading differently, even though your head is telling you it's a new season for the organization. A friend of mine founded a successful nonprofit and hired a capable and talented replacement; however, this founder told me in a moment of candor that he couldn't envision himself staying longer than a month for that very reason.

I believe my scenario, and that of my friend, underscore that if you have a defined role within the organization, you can be a valuable resource for your successor. If you don't, it would be better if you left.

Another important principle is to give advice to my successor only when asked. I have done this well at times and not so well at others. But this discipline needs to be the rule rather than the exception. The successor does need historical context in decision-making, but ideally that is best done through the board of directors. This underscores the need to have a minimum of 50 percent of board members with institutional knowledge, especially in the early post-transition days.

Although I had the energy to delay the transition process for two to three years, I wanted energy to help John with this transition and also have the bandwidth for the "next season" of God's calling on my life.

### A NEW CHAPTER

When we decided to name this book, "Founding to Finishing," I was a little hesitant about the word "Finishing." Although it references the tenure of an organizational leader, there is a subtle inference that there is not another "founding" on the horizon—not necessarily an organizational founding, but rather a founding of new purpose.

Our lives are by nature a continual founding to finishing if we are open to God's creative plan. The finishing is, in some ways, just the end of a chapter and

SEASON THREE: FINISHING

not the end of the book. What *is* consistent is our "why" and the tangible expression of that why as it unfolds in our future endeavors.

The most purposeful people I know have lived in this way. May it be so for us as well.

> ### KEY LESSON
>
> The "baton pass" is crucial to a successful transition. Just as important is the design and execution of "what's next" for the outgoing executive director. Have clear boundaries for your role during and after the transition. Only give advice when asked. If the founder has a future role within the organization, make sure it is clearly defined.
>
> *How can your experience and skills benefit others beyond your role as a founder?*

# EPILOGUE

I HOPE this book has been helpful in your journey to serve others. It is amazing how just a few "nuggets" of advice can enhance and redirect a mission.

As you have read these chapters, it's my hope that you were able to discover some suggestions that will make your organization more effective for those you serve.

It is an honor to share some insights with you about my Eagle Ranch journey. Our mission at Eagle Ranch continues to evolve as will yours. Having an ongoing posture of learning is so important to maintaining relevancy. It is even more important to be good stewards of that to which we have been called.

Our heart at Eagle Ranch is to help others help others. To that end, we have ongoing opportunities through our Wings Consulting initiative for those who wish to go deeper into some of the insights in this book. For more information, please reach out to me personally at estaub@eagleranch.org.

God's blessings to you in the journey ahead.

EDWIN J. STAUB
*Founder, Eagle Ranch*

# Resources and References

Eagle Ranch, www.eagleranch.org

The Wings Center, www.thewingscenter.org

Robert Woodruff, Former CEO and Chairman, Coca-Cola Company.

Vince Dooley, Former Head Football Coach, University of Georgia.

George Mueller, Founder of the Ashley Down Orphanage in England.

Tim Irwin, PhD., Mark Albers. *Impact: Great Leadership Changes Everything.* BenBella Books, 1991.

Dr. Tim Irwin. *Extraordinary Influence: How Great Leaders Bring Out the Best in Others.* Gildan Media, 2018.

Dallas Willard. "Living in the Vision of God." Essay, DallasWillard.org.

Dietrich Bonhoeffer. *Life Together: The Classic Exploration of Christian Community.* HarperOne, 1949.

Jim Collins, Jerry I. Porras. *Built to Last.* HarperBusiness, 1994.

Clayton M. Christensen, James Allworth, et al. "How Will You Measure Your Life." *Harvard Business Review*, 2010.

Pat MacMillan. *Mission Centered Governance.* The Maclellan Foundation, 2004/2020.

Jeffrey Sonnenfeld. *The Hero's Farewell: What Happens When CEOs Retire.* Oxford University Press, 1991.

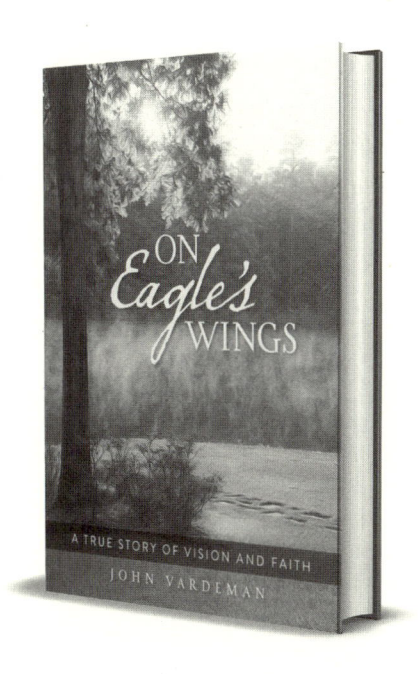

IN its 12th printing, *On Eagle's Wings* is the compelling story of two young men from very different worlds. Their lives are inextricably linked by the founding in 1985 of Eagle Ranch, one of the nation's most progressive therapeutic Christian homes for needy boys.

*On Eagle's Wings* is an inspiring confirmation of the power of human perseverance and God's unconditional love and limitless grace. It is a must-read that is sure to touch your heart.

To purchase a copy of *On Eagle's Wings*, contact Eagle Ranch at info@eagleranch.org.